"Gary Unger has had a career that can be a model for others hoping for a successful life in architecture and interior design. His new book, *Your Architecture Career*, is a very useful addition to the very limited bibliography of books on this important subject. It should be on every young architect's and interior designer's personal bookshelf."

—Bradford Perkins, FAIA, chairman and CEO of Perkins Eastman Architects, coauthor of *Architect's Essentials of Starting, Assessing, and Transitioning a Design Firm*

"Gary Unger's book, *Your Architecture Career*, is an insightful look into the past, present, and future of the profession. . . . He skillfully examines the tension in the profession between art, technology, and business. The book is a good splash of realism for young minds beginning in the profession and will give them a jump-start on their careers. It will fill how-to-do-it gaps for a seasoned practitioner. It's a fun read for anyone with the faintest interest in the design and construction industry."

—Chuck Thomsen, FAIA, former chairman of 3DI, creator of the "fast track construction scheduling" concept, and author of *Program Management 2.0* and *Managing Brainpower*

"By sharing with readers his diverse professional experiences, personal knowledge, and extensive management expertise, Gary Unger has created a richly textured narrative about all aspects of an architectural career as well as a highly practical, detailed guide for aspiring architects and architectural firms."

—Roger K. Lewis, FAIA, professor emeritus, University of Maryland, and author of *Architect? A Candid Guide to the Profession*

"*Your Architecture Career* provides important information and helpful tips for those launching a career in architecture, emerging professionals, and experienced architects. Topics include starting and progressing in a career in architecture, excelling in a career position, and the process of starting a firm with much detail."

—Lee W. Waldrep, PhD, author of *Becoming an Architect: A Guide to Careers in Design*

"Many times, I have sat at a table opposite Gary Unger as he led a team through an innovative design, beginning with a goal. In *Your Architecture Career*, Gary leads you through your most important design to your most important goal—your career as an architect."

—Joel Rollins, AV technologist and futurist, host of *The Week* on rAVe Radio

"In *Your Architecture Career*, Gary Unger presents unique insights collected from a successful career as the founder and leader of Stamford-based architecture firm CPG. The practical guidelines within this manual would be invaluable to anyone hoping to follow Gary's lead in having a successful and fulfilling professional life."

—Doug Winshall, founder of ClearRock Properties

YOUR ARCHITECTURE CAREER

YOUR ARCHITECTURE CAREER

HOW TO BUILD A SUCCESSFUL PROFESSIONAL LIFE

GARY UNGER

ALLWORTH PRESS
NEW YORK

Allworth Press books may be purchased in bulk at special discounts for sales promotion, corporate gifts, fund-raising, or educational purposes. Special editions can also be created to specifications. For details, contact the Special Sales Department, Allworth Press, 307 West 36th Street, 11th Floor, New York, NY 10018 or info@skyhorsepublishing.com.

23 22 21 20 19   5 4 3 2 1

Published by Allworth Press, an imprint of Skyhorse Publishing, Inc., 307 West 36th Street, 11th Floor, New York, NY 10018. Allworth Press® is a registered trademark of Skyhorse Publishing, Inc.®, a Delaware corporation.

www.allworth.com

Cover design by Mary Ann Smith
Cover art by adimas/AdobeStock and Vladitto/Adobestock

Library of Congress Cataloging-in-Publication Data
Names: Unger, Gary, author.
Title: Your architecture career: how to build a successful professional life/Gary Unger.
Description: New York : Allworth Press, an imprint of Skyhorse Publishing,
    Inc., 2018. | Includes bibliographical references and index.
Identifiers: LCCN 2017058989 (print) | LCCN 2017059319 (ebook) | ISBN
    9781621536352 (ebook) | ISBN 9781621536345 (hardcover: alk. paper)
Subjects: LCSH: Architecture—Vocational guidance.
Classification: LCC NA1995 (ebook) | LCC NA1995 .U54 2018 (print) | DDC
    720.23—dc23
LC record available at https://lccn.loc.gov/2017058989

Hardcover ISBN: 978-1-62153-634-5
Paperback ISBN: 978-1-62153-702-1
eBook ISBN: 978-1-62153-635-2

Printed in the United States of America

Dedication

I dedicate this to my mom, who passed away at 101 while I was writing this book.

To my dad for encouraging me to pursue the practice of architecture and to convince me to stay the course during my dreadful freshman year at Washington University.

To Mom for taking an extreme interest in my career when I started my firm by asking questions about each new client, about our design concepts and new ways of working.

I am so grateful for my family's considerable sacrifices to provide the funds that allowed me to finish six years of architecture school debt-free. Dad was an accomplished planner and treasurer of Prudential Insurance Company, and he surely needed to use all his skills to keep me in line.

To my wife, Betsey, for giving me the encouragement to start my own venture and for helping me for the first 10 years set policies and employee programs that have endured the test of time for our 35 years.

I would also like to recognize very special employees who have passed and played major roles in the firm's success:

Dennis Tardy
Karina Saari
Dean Forst
Roger Morris
Carl Mirbach

A Note to Readers

This book is intended to inspire:

- Students in their last two years at a college or university studying architecture and interior design
- Seniors or recent graduates who are looking for their first job in an architectural or interior design office
- Those who are already working at an architectural or interior design firm or at a company in a corporate real estate or facilities management capacity
- Everyone who is considering starting his or her own architectural or interior design firm
- Clients who might find inspiration and understanding from the ideas I share
- Realtors, owner's reps, project managers, and all other project consultants

I also hope this book will enable professionals to make their journey in architecture more successful, more enriching, and, most important, more profitable.

If I can just reach one student, one architect, or one owner, inspiring them to have a more satisfying career, then I will consider this book a success.

Table of Contents

Foreword

I wish this book were available when I was in school. It would have made my last two years in architecture school much more productive and my initial search for the "best job" so much easier. The concepts presented represent clear thinking with practical experiences for all to follow throughout their career to maximize their potential for success.

Most "self-help" books are read, then put on a shelf, never to be opened again. *Your Architecture Career* is a book that should be kept close by for easy reference. What is nice about this book is that it is well organized for the reader to follow as their career progresses.

It is a great reference book for those just starting out and impresses upon the student/intern/architect the importance of being aware of their career opportunities. It is easy to come back to chapters to review specifics, to share ideas, or test one's own development.

I think of this book as being similar to current "Kickstarter" programs designed for those bringing a new product or service to the marketplace. We all need a boost when we are starting out—Kickstarter programs give entrepreneurs the *financial* boost they need. *Your Architectural Career* gives professionals the *career* boost they need with tried and tested ways of working to succeed in the world of architecture.

I describe how the process of architecture and interior design is similar to a relay race and how important "handoffs" are for both the individual and the firm. Being a good team player is being a great architect. The other theme I describe is the benefit of being a strategic partner with your client—not just a "good vendor."

I will definitely recommend this book to schools, students, interns, architects, and firm owners as a guide to helping professionals enjoy and prosper in this wonderful profession.

—Gary Unger
2018

Introduction

To each new employee we bring into the firm, no matter what level or discipline, we give a detailed orientation of our processes, procedures, likes, dislikes, and most of all the unique ways in which we deal with our clients.

Since our business divides into three primary parts, so does our orientation to new employees:

1. Business Practices/Professional Practice
2. Marketing and Client Relationships
3. Design Goals

This book deals primarily with items 1 and 2—Business Practices / Professional Practice and Marketing and Client Relationships. In my mind, each of the three parts is weighted equally, and if one or two parts are weak, the entire firm will suffer.

The curriculum in most architecture schools focuses on Design with minimal academic time spent on Professional Practice in the last semester of the final year. This is a huge problem for firms looking for talent that can grow quickly into management positions.

I decided to write this book because I could not find a book on Professional Practice that I could use in my business that approached these issues from the point of view of the student, the employee, and the business owner. When I searched for books used by universities in their professional practice courses, I found that schools used books that were out of date or completely off message, and some did not even use a textbook. They relied on professors' notes from personal experience.

Your Architecture Career is a comprehensive guide, full of tips for recent graduates, interns starting out, and owners of architectural businesses, that offers a better chance to excel and rise up quickly through the ranks in a very tough profession.

I include tips that will help you succeed. **Look for the "TIP" graphic.** Yes, it is true that experience is one of the best teachers, but sharing with you what I learned from the jobs I have had, as well as thousands of projects done by my firm, will help jump start your career.

I have written this book from the perspective that few are taught to consider the process from the client's point of view. This book will give you a competitive advantage by helping you understand how your client thinks and what your client needs.

For seven years, prior to starting CPG Architects, I was the client. I was Director of Worldwide Planning and Design for American Express. Only when you are on the inside can you appreciate the difference between the needs, attitude, and responsibilities of the architectural firm and the corporate person responsible for facilities. The architectural firm has one client, whereas the internal corporate project manager often has multiple clients.

The book is also about helping architects understand that when you have options, you should first try to think them through from your client's point of view. I write about the importance of acting as a *strategic partner* to the client, not just being a good vendor.

It is important that even those whose primary focus is on the design aspect of the profession take the time to understand and appreciate all the other steps involved in getting the work, managing the client, dealing with time, and finally, handling the money.

I hope this book is also valuable to other prime project players such as realtors, owner's reps, project managers, facility managers, and, yes, even your clients. It is only when each group understands that the practice of architecture is a team sport managing a series of handoffs, just like a baton is handed off from runner to runner in a relay race, that you will appreciate and respect the idiosyncrasies of one another's business.

It is exciting to be sharing my experiences and knowledge with you. I welcome your feedback and appreciate the opportunity to offer all I have learned from my own work experiences and interviews with other architects and related service providers, as well as the insights I have gained from reading numerous excellent books, which I refer to from time to time.

Debunking Three Myths about Architecture and Architects
(There are many.)

Having preconceived ideas usually makes it difficult to think about new ideas with an open mind. Clearing the air about these myths will give you a better chance to follow through with testing new personal growth concepts. I have prepared responses to often-shared myths. While others may have different experiences, I hope thinking about the positive possibilities in architecture will make it easier for you to pursue your dreams.

MYTH #1: "YOU CAN'T MAKE MONEY AS AN ARCHITECT"

False! You can make a great living as an architect, either as an employee or as an owner. You might not make as much as the very few that hit home runs in the dot-com businesses, or those we hear about who create start-up ventures that get sold for huge numbers of dollars, many even without a revenue stream.

You can make an excellent living, have loads of fun, put your kids through college debt-free, and have a healthy retirement. For all those who hit home runs by going public or selling out, we know there any many more that go bust. These entrepreneurs are the type who will keep trying time after time.

I can tell you from experience: it just takes a little planning, personal goal setting, and loads of luck to have a very comfortable life in the field of architecture. The ones who hit the home runs have also had some luck.

Plan the course. This book will help you understand how to make the best of your options, realize opportunities, and take advantage of luck that comes along.

MYTH #2: "YOU NEED TO BE AN ARTIST TO BECOME AN ARCHITECT"

False! I am definitely not an artist, and I can tell you, firsthand, most architects are not artists. Do not mistake what I am saying. Being able to draw well will give you a leg up against the competition. But it is not a requirement.

My first-year freehand drawing professor spoke plainly with the bright-eyed freshmen. His desire to shock us worked; he came right out and said to the entire class, "If you are not an artist, you should forget about being an architect." I was devastated and ready to quit. It was only because my father drove from Houston to St. Louis and talked me out of quitting that I was able to stay the course and have a wonderful career. I was never as talented a freehand artist as many of the others, but I persevered and eventually succeeded in many other aspects of the curriculum.

MYTH #3: "ARCHITECTS NEED TO WORK NONSTOP TO BE SUCCESSFUL"

False! It is true that most architects work crazy hours, but it does not have to be that way. Now that I have been around the business and clients for many years, I think there are many ways to offset the prime reasons architects work long hours:

1. Most architects starting out feel they need to do too much themselves. For the three prime parts of the business—marketing, design, and finance—the architect needs to find temps, consultants, or trusted employees to share the workload. Trying to do it all yourself is a surefire way to fail.
2. Most projects start too late, causing schedules that do not allow for the proper amount of time for each set of tasks and resulting in projects that run on overtime.
3. Projects that start tasks out of phase often result in the redoing of previously prepared steps. We call this "churn." Churn kills profitability, induces stress, and causes mistakes. Architects should prepare and maintain the project schedule to maintain sanity.
4. For many designers, the design process is never over. It is admirable to want to explore all options to produce the perfect

solution, but if the design phase is not properly managed, the loss of time will be felt in all the succeeding phases.

One of the primary goals of this book is to help you to master the business part of the profession so you will have a balanced work, family, and personal life.

PART I

Finishing School and Getting a Job

CHAPTER 1

Completing Architecture School

WHAT TO FOCUS ON DURING YOUR LAST TWO YEARS

Most course curricula become very specific in the last two years of an architectural or interior design program—without a lot of room for electives. Here are three things I encourage all students to focus on during their years in school:

Additional Elective Courses

Despite the rigors of the required design/thesis lab courses, I recommend taking as many professional practice or business administration courses as you can fit in. This will be your last and probably only time to be exposed to the foundation of the business of architecture. Not all of you will become primary designers in the firm you choose to work for, so having more than a basic understanding of the specifics of the business will be useful. For example, it is necessary to learn all you can about finance, marketing concepts, proposal writing, presentation techniques, time management, and project management.

Courses on Creative Writing

Architects need to write more than they think they will. It is imperative that architects take as many courses on creative writing as they can fit into their schedule. If there is a course on email writing, I encourage you to take it because the state of email communication in business today is pathetic. It is one thing if you are writing an email to a friend asking to get together for lunch and it is not worded properly, but it is another when you send a client an email about a schedule slippage, budget overrun, or other detail. Emails should be written like letters with a beginning, middle, and end. Most important of all, *do not forget emails are legal documents.*

Creating a Contact "Job Search" Database

Start while you are in school to create a contact list of professors, students, school administration staff, visiting professors, potential companies you may send résumés to, vendors, and speakers.

One of the most important tasks you will learn in Part 1 is how to get organized for an effective job search.

The list will be valuable to you in school and for many years to come as you begin your professional career.

My recommendation is to keep your job search references and information separate from your personal phone contact list.

There are many templates available for tracking this information using Excel or Google Docs. There are also free and inexpensive database apps that will keep you organized.

Important information to track

- Contact Name
  - Title
  - Business Affiliation
  - Business Phone
- Company Name
  - Additional Contact
  - Address
- Date Résumé Submitted
- How Résumé Submitted
- What Was Submitted
  - Letter
  - Résumé
- Follow-Up Date
- Result
- Job Description
  - Personal Notes

- Cell Phone
- Email
- Type of Contact

- Main Phone #
- Website

- References

- Interview Notes

IMPRESSING YOUR PROFESSORS SO THEY WILL REMEMBER AND RECOMMEND YOU

Many of the professors at Washington University School of Architecture, which I attended, were very successful architects in their home countries. It was fashionable for schools during the '60s to use visiting professors. Many had both professional and personal reasons for coming, beyond their contracted teaching assignments. Teaching was a way for them to take a year and travel through the United States. Many also had special design projects they needed to complete, or were doing research for future books, so having access to loads of students they did not have to pay was very positive. This was both a plus and a minus to me. The plus was that I was able to help them with those tasks, and it was a great way to learn about real projects. The minus was that they were super busy and did not have extra time to meet for discussion and advice beyond the assigned lab period. If you find yourself in this position, volunteer in order to get an opportunity to develop the relationship and hopefully a recommendation.

Professors are excellent references once they know your capabilities. In order to make that happen, go out of your way to volunteer to help and chat with them about their firms. Take the time to look them up online so you can better understand their practice. Without being too pushy, ask for their advice and support.

NETWORKING WITH CLASSMATES, ALUMNI, AND PROFESSORS

Coordinate your job search research with classmates and share information with one another about firms in various cities. When you start looking for your first job, there is a lot of information to gather, and the "divide and conquer" approach makes a lot of sense, especially with the more mundane tasks of gathering contact information about firms in each city.

By the middle of your next-to-last year, you need to be making contacts for summer jobs. Your professors should be able to be a big help to you in the search. If you have a placement office or guidance office, sometimes they get calls from local firms or associations like the AIA and ASID and know who is looking for summer interns. I have always considered alumni to be the best resource because there should be an immediate bond with them and, hopefully, willingness to help. At least a good letter should get you in the door for an interview with one or more of the alumni from your school.

CHAPTER 2

Deciding on a Career Path

A SUMMER INTERNSHIP BEFORE YOUR LAST YEAR

The summer of your next-to-last year in architecture school is one of the most important for your future career as an architect. If you are able to land a summer internship, it will significantly enhance your ability to find a job after graduation. Employers reviewing résumés for a full-time job like to know that you have had some related work experience. I recommend starting to look for that summer job in February or March. Use your connections to help you find out about potential summer jobs. You need to learn how to leverage your relationships with:

- Professors, school counselors, and alumni coordinators
- Family friends and students
- Architectural alumni
- Local AIA contacts—get to know the staff in local AIA offices

I am not big on following or responding to job boards, want ads, or online recruiters. In my experience, summer jobs are rarely listed that way. You need to be looking for the job that is not posted. It is to your advantage that summertime is the biggest period for employee vacations. In many cases, your job may be filling in for employees who are on vacation. Your cover letter or email should trigger ideas in the mind of the reader that it would be a good idea to have you fill in for someone on vacation. Listing what you can do for the firm is critical. Do not just say you are looking for a summer job. Firms always have loads of fill-in projects, but often they do not want to take full-time employees away from billable work. In your letter or email, suggest that you can help by:

- Updating drawing templates and standard detail sheets
- Helping with the firms' social media program—blog, website, LinkedIn, Facebook, Snapchat, etc. For many firms these are not updated on a consistent basis.
- Updating standard forms
- Updating the library: catalogues, materials, and finishes
- Updating presentation graphics
- Assisting with measuring buildings/spaces
- Drawing base plans/Doing area calculations
- Doing renderings with SketchUp or Revit

Most of the time, the summer job will either be in the city where you are going to school or where you live—this narrows down your search and hopefully makes it easier.

The letter or email you write to a prospective firm does not have to include a formal list of other work experiences unless you have had other appropriate jobs that you think are beneficial to include. A well-written letter is sufficient.

The letter needs to include a few basics:

1. Address the letter to someone—not *To Whom It May Concern*.
2. Say in the letter how you heard of them. Compliment their website.
3. Describe the summer job you are looking for. Include the period you can work—especially the start date.

WHEN AND HOW TO START LOOKING FOR A FULL-TIME JOB DURING YOUR LAST YEAR

I recommend you start looking for your first full-time job in January or February of your last year of architecture school. Now it is time to get serious with your job search. You definitely want to beat the crowd. Finding an opportunity and negotiating your salary and start time takes a while, especially if you are looking for work in a city where you have to travel for the interview. When you contact firms, it is important to include suggested dates when you are available for the interview.

Unless you are very lucky and you already have a job waiting for you, you will learn that the process of finding a job is as important as knowing your stuff. Once again, firms do not advertise for beginning jobs, so the jobs you see advertised will often be for more experienced positions.

During your last two years, leverage your relationships with:

- Professors
- School counselors and alumni coordinators
- Family friends
- Students
- Vendors who come in to speak
- Architectural alumni
- Local AIA contacts
- Builders and developers

Relationships happen in the most unforeseen and unexpected ways. Just casually mentioning you are getting ready to look for a job may elicit positive comments from people you do not expect can help.

There are a number of key decisions you will make that will influence the kind of job you are looking for, such as:

- Where do you want to live?
- What type of firm do you want to work for?
- What kind of architecture would you like to do?

JOB SEARCH CHECKLIST: WHAT SHOULD YOU LOOK FOR IN A FIRM?

Look through the following checklists and mark your answers. Once you finish the checklist, review your responses. This will help clarify the kind of community, and firm, where you may want to work for your first job after architecture school.

It also makes sense to share these lists and your responses with friends, professors, and vendors you have met. You will be surprised how many people can help if they know the type of work you are interested in and where you might like to locate. Your professors will have a large database of contacts and if asked should be willing to help. Learn to leverage all your friends and contacts and be sure to help them if asked. Many of those you have met will be willing to write an introductory letter for you. I have said this before: use your campus career center and alumni officers—they are very important.

Where Do You Want to Live?

Most of today's students look for either summer or full-time jobs in the city where they went to school or the city where they live or grew up. These are choices that are more familiar; however, those looking more broadly may follow the ideas below:

- New England
- Mid-Atlantic
- South
- Southwest
- West
- Midwest

- Large urban center
- Suburban
- Small town
- Rural
- University community
- Cultural center
- Area with outdoor living opportunities
- Area with sports focus

Architectural opportunities and development change in cities as economic conditions rise and fall. If you are interested primarily in residential design, keep abreast of corporate growth patterns, especially for the high-end projects. In stronger economies, the high-end residential second-home and vacation market increases in cities catering to outdoor activities. If, on the other hand, you are interested more in the design of commercial development projects, watch for cities with strong economic incentive programs and downtown redevelopment projects. Cities that have incentive programs to attract corporations also bring growth to firms that do architecture or interiors.

What Type of Firm Do You Want to Work For?

It often takes a few job experiences to figure out what type of firm fits you the best:

- Large international
- Large domestic
- Multioffice
- Regional

- Specialist by type of work
- General practice
- Sole-proprietor
- Local

Each of the firm types offers very different experiences. You will find that not only are the types and sizes of projects very different, the types of staff employed are also very different. For instance, when I started my first job with Harrison and Abramovitz, I was assigned to the New York City opera building project that had started a few years prior to my joining and would continue a few more years before construction started. It takes a certain type of person to want to make a total personal commitment to one project. Being tethered to a desk for years was not my idea of an exciting career. Conversely, when I joined CRS Architects in New York City, most of their work was outside the City and I knew I would be doing a lot of traveling. For me, being in a position to meet new clients of all types was exciting. The office was alive as I watched teams prepare to go out to work on projects, and then when they came back from a squatters[1]/charrette and we would hear about their experiences. I loved to travel and be in a trusted position to represent the firm in the field.

What Kind of Architecture Would You Like to Do?

Starting out, many students are looking for firms that have a general practice and do many different types of projects, to give them a broad orientation to the practice. Others may already have an idea what they are looking for and start out with a firm that has a specialty, such as one of the following:

- Commercial
- Corporate
- Retail
- Residential
- Entertainment
- Cultural
- Sports

- Green
- Heavy timber
- High rise
- Health care
- Education
- Hospitals
- Public/Government

Knowing What I Know Now

If I could start all over, knowing what I know now, I would go for a midsize architectural firm with forty to sixty-five staff that had a history of award-winning projects and a management team of three or more principals where each was responsible for marketing, design, or operations. I would look for a firm with a varied client list with obvious repeat business. Selecting a design-oriented firm fits my personality because I know I am a much better manager than a designer and can shine in that type of environment. I appreciate great design and know project management can be just as creative and appreciated.

---

1 "Squatters" refers to architects who move in to a client's office for a period of time to do a specific task. This is a term we coined at CRS Architects.

A firm of 40–65 employees should have a mix of large and small projects with a percentage of work in town and out of town, allowing for some travel. In addition, that size firm is large enough to be able to employ specialists in each field and have the bench strength to be competitive for larger projects. Smaller high design firms, without the obvious bench strength, may do great work but often have a harder time capturing the larger assignments. Firms larger than 50–75 often divide the work into studios where each studio tends to work on one or two types of projects. It may not be as efficient for the firm, but I like the opportunity to work on many project types during the year. The opportunity for repeat business is also positive. Repeat business projects tend to be smaller, which I like because they usually go faster. The mixture of "out of the ground" architectural projects, interior design, planning, and design projects would provide a positive combination.

The point I made about firms having at least three principals is based on my feeling that businesses of this size with serious revenue potential have unique responsibilities that require at least one person dedicated to each of the major parts of the business. That does not preclude overlap in project management, marketing, and presentations.

Finally, firms of this size will probably be in a larger city with access to good housing stock and extensive educational and cultural activities.

Getting into the HR details

The human resources and financial factors I list below cross all business types and are not specific to architecture or interior design. The list always seems to get longer as each generation passes through the business cycles, and some of these items are more important when you are single and fancy-free, married, married with children, or moving on in age and looking for greater security.

- Base salary
- Bonus
- 401K
- Regular salary reviews
- Working hours
- Vacation/Time off
- Sick days/Personal days

- Medical insurance
- Life insurance/Disability
- Job title
- Paid training programs
- Assistance with the ARE (Architect Registration Exam)

When I started CPG Architects, I was 38 years old and married with two young boys, so each of the items in this list was important to me. We made the point of addressing each issue and developed guidelines as though it would also be important to anyone who joined the firm.

Salaries and benefits make up over 90 percent of service firms' expenses, and while it makes good business sense to watch every penny, being shortsighted can cost the firm more in terms of absenteeism, productivity, churn, and potential recruitment. There is a minimum firms must provide to employees to be competitive in each marketplace, and the minimum changes constantly depending on the type of firm, size of firm, location of firm, and the general economy and demand for talent.

Our firm has always tried to provide salaries and benefits at the higher end of the scale because in the final analysis our only assets are the folks who work for us. They are our "product" and our "representatives." They are what make us efficient and profitable. When owners think of themselves first as employees, rather than being special and entitled to additional benefits, the firm performs more effectively. Word spreads very quickly from firm to firm as to the way employees are treated.

As we get older and perhaps have families, our priorities change; however, our policies and offerings should not change. All firms should have a simple and direct employee manual that clearly spells out policy. Like all policy, there is often need for clarification or compromise. In recent years, we have introduced flexible working hours, work-at-home options, and new technology to enhance workplace strategies and have used discretion at times for those injured or sick who fall out of standard. It is necessary to be flexible where circumstances demand flexibility and necessary to have explicit guidelines so employees can follow the rules.

An employee manual and handbook is a requirement for all firms. Lifelong jobs, as my dad had, are outdated. Employees today think in terms of "career for me" not "career for life."

CHAPTER 3

Landing Your First Job

PREPARING YOUR RÉSUMÉ

There is an enormous amount of material online, in articles, and in books advising you as to the best way to prepare a résumé. I will focus on just the few things I like to see.

I don't expect to see a lot of relevant experience when someone has just graduated, but I still think the résumé can demonstrate professionalism even when sharing experiences about summer work or school projects.

Looking for a job is similar to a firm looking for a new client. Here are some of the similarities:

- Both are very tough, especially in tough economic times
- Both take a lot of hard, focused work
- Both require you to rely on all of your contacts for help
- Both require you to be creative about the way you present yourself
- Both require practice
- Both require you to make a *perfect* first impression

A résumé shouldn't just be rushed out to prospective employers; here are some key things to think about in preparation:

1. The experiences you have had, especially those summer jobs. Describe what you did, what you learned, and how you excelled. What do you think you are best at? What are you passionate about? You might also be asked: What *don't* you like to do?
   a. On a *professional* level, consider if you are good at managing others, design, selecting materials, using technology, or freehand drawing.

    b. On a *personal* level, think about what you like in terms of music, food, freehand drawing, photography, travel, etc.

2. What other skills do you have that are needed by architectural and interior design firms? I hope that you can say that you have first-rate writing skills, technical skills, or other skills in areas such as communicating, rendering, website design, or social media such as Facebook, LinkedIn, or Twitter. Firms like beginners who are multitalented so they are able to fill in as needed.

3. Being creative with your résumé format is fine. Just do not be cute with fonts, text sizes, and colors. Keep your résumé very professional. Résumés are often printed out and passed around the office, so a colorful résumé printed on a black-and-white printer may be difficult to read.

4. There is no telling how your résumé will be viewed, so keep the formatting simple. Try sending it to friends who have different types of smartphones, iPads, tablets, and computers. It is best to send it in a .pdf format, as phones and computers view it with all variations of software.

5. Ask friends to print it to check the formatting. Make sure there is not a blank last page.

YOUR JOB SEARCH SHOULD INCLUDE SIX PARTS

1. Cover Letter

Never address a résumé "To Whom It May Concern." Call the company to get a name.

2. One-Page Résumé

- Name, e-mail, and cell number on top. Your address is not as important and may be distracting if where you are now is not where you are going.
- Include a short summary of personal goals and objectives, 3–4 lines.

- Include only your higher education, starting with the most recent.
- Work history with dates, starting with most recent. Each experience should focus on your responsibilities and what you learned and perhaps how you benefited others.
- Describe your technical skills and awards. REVIT is currently a hot subject, and in the next few years, even the smaller firms will be well into virtual reality to stay competitive. If you're trained in this, make sure to let prospective employers know.
- List extracurricular activities, interests, and accomplishments such as continuing education, courses like Dale Carnegie leadership training, or courses taken in associations such as the AIA, IFMA, ASID, or LEED.

Very Important: With data and internet security high in most firms, understand that companies do not like opening attachments. Be clear in the email that the .pdf attachment is your résumé or, better yet, copy and paste it in the body of the email. Test opening and printing it prior to sending.

On the following pages is an example of a very simple résumé format that reads well:

Gary Unger   **gary_unger@cpgarch.com**
203-274-2685   **www.cpgarch.com**

Summary

After transferring ownership of CPG to three employees, I am exploring ways to give back to the architectural profession that has been so good to me over my fifty-year career. One half century is a long time to have such a positive career experience.

I am in the process of publishing a book titled *Your Architecture Career*, dedicated to helping kids in architectural and interior design school, interns starting out, and architects in practice become more successful, more quickly.

I am starting a free consulting business to help corporations manage project risk by improving the RFP process, developing checklists to improve milestone handoffs, and defining lean procedures to improve vendor profitability.

Education

1964–1966	University of Texas	Bachelor of Architecture
1960–1964	Washington University	Bachelor of Science in Architecture

Experience

1990–Present   **Founder of Link Systems**   Stamford, CT

Link Systems is a software developer specializing in designing applications for the Real Estate industry. Applications are for Lease Management, Facility Management, Maintenance/Work Order and Portfolio Management for Building Owners and Property Managers. Over 900 major corporations use Link Systems products.

1980–Present   **Founder of CPG Architects**   Stamford, CT

CPG has designed thousands of architectural and interior design projects in the Tri-state area for corporations, municipalities, and healthcare and educational institutions. We focus on designing facilities that are beautiful as well as functional and efficient.

1974–1980   **Director of Worldwide Planning and Design for American Express**

Initially managed the planning and design of Amex's 1.2 million-square-foot headquarters tower in NYC, then stayed on for five more years to manage facilities worldwide. Amex owned or leased 3,500 properties worldwide.

1968–1974   **Associate with Caudill Rowlett Scott Architects**

Without a doubt CRS was the best architectural firm in the country to learn about the "right way" to deliver client services. Bill Caudill taught his employees to be more than good architects and service providers. He taught us how to be strategic partners.

Awards/Skills

March of Dimes Real Estate Person of the Year (2010). Successfully developed skills in marketing, presentation techniques, long-range planning, business forecasting, and organizational development.

Interests

Travel, motorcycle racing, antique cars, sculpture, museums

3. Preparing Your Portfolio

Because architecture is a visual discipline, selecting a portfolio is an important consideration. You need to think about the design of the case you will be using as well as the format of the material you intend to show.

Because your portfolio has different purposes, and will be seen by different audiences, it needs to be flexible so it can easily be well organized. Label your work to indicate if work was for a course assignment, completed independent, or for another firm. It is useful to know when the work was completed and the approximate amount of time involved. Students should document and preserve all their work.

Your portfolio is a design statement and reflects your design personality and organizational capabilities. I definitely recommend avoiding a portfolio case where artwork is inserted in a loose manner. The work can be mixed up and out of order, and there goes your story. On the other extreme, a hardbound version is also inflexible and inappropriate.

My recommendation is for you to use a three-ring binder or the two-stud attachment method. This type of a portfolio is best because you can reorganize your story for any audience. An 11 × 17-inch seems to be the most flexible format.

4. Portfolio

I recommend you do not imbed examples of your portfolio with the résumé. It may become too large for a server to accept, or it may be difficult to print. You could provide a link to your personal website or have an online portfolio—that way you can continually update it and control the way it is used. Often candidates are asked to leave their portfolio so it can be shared with others. Try to avoid doing this; rather, say you would be pleased to come back to show it again when the person is available. Things get lost.

5. Getting the Interview

Be prepared with the best story about yourself and your background for the audience you are meeting with. You should always take the time to research the company you are meeting with before you go so you have the information you need to compose your most focused narrative.

Understand:

- What is the company's history?
- Where did the founders go to school?

- What type of work do they do?
- Do they have a specialty?
- What type of clients do they work for?
- Does it look like they are getting a lot of repeat business?
- Does their website talk about their employee policies?

Remember, when you are interviewing at a company, or just showing your portfolio to someone who is going to give you advice, it is all about *your story* and very little about your work.

The advice I always give to anyone making a presentation is that you are most often judged, in the following order, by:

1. Your appearance
2. How you speak
3. What you say

The smaller the firm you are interviewing with, the higher-level person you are most likely to meet with and the fewer number of interviews you may have before you know if they want you, or if you like them. Going back for multiple interviews is tough and time-consuming but necessary when interviewing with larger firms.

For advertised positions, you may be interviewing with a recruiter who screens applicants prior to sending them to the firm, or you may be meeting with HR. In those cases, he or she will be looking to see if you are a good fit, and, if so, then you will meet with a key person in the firm so they can find out what you know.

6. Follow-Up

Always send a thank-you note, follow-up letter, or email after your meeting. Remember—most résumés are looked at for about 6–10 seconds and immediately are sorted by "keep for follow-up" or "discard."

I first look at the cover letter, then the résumé itself: education/degree, personal statement, and the last job or two listed. I think the cover letter is the most important part of the packet because it shows what research you have done on the firm.

There may be a new trend starting—accepting video introductions.

WHAT TO WEAR TO INTERVIEWS

If you know with whom you will be meeting, you can ask about dress code, or you can go to the firm's website to see if there are employee photos. If there are, look over those photos and consider, "How are they dressed?" A good rule of thumb is to be dressed one level *above* your interviewer. If you do not know with whom you will be meeting, you can always call the firm and ask the person answering the phone about the dress code. Another option is to look at the firm's Facebook page to see if there are any photos, or read posts or blogs that may help you to understand more about its culture.

WHERE YOU MAY BE INTERVIEWED

At my firm, we hold interviews in any number of locations, depending upon the level of the interview and the other meetings underway. The location depends upon whether the interviewer wants you to see the inner workings of the office or to just stay in the public areas. At my firm, if the office is busy, we might stay in the reception area and chat at a table, or we might meet in the lounge or café or go to one of the conference rooms.

The location for your interview also depends on the number of people attending the interview. I like to have at least one other employee with me for the interview; two others are preferable. For that reason, you have to be ready for any situation. Bring a few extra résumés with you.

QUESTIONS YOU MAY BE ASKED

Here are just a few of the questions you may be asked in a typical interview. You might want to prepare how you would answer any or all of these questions in advance:

1. Did you look at our website? What did you think?
2. How did you hear about us?
3. Why did you want to interview with us?
4. What do you like about our work?
5. What type of work are you most interested in?
6. What did you like most about your summer jobs?
7. What are your outside interests?
8. What are you most interested in: design or management?
9. What were your biggest successes and failures in school?
10. What will you bring to our firm?

Before you apply to a firm, and certainly before you go to your interview, make sure all your personal social media sites are "clean" of any objectionable material. Your future employer will probably look you up—it is so easy. Do a search on your name to see what is out there in the cloud for all to view.

QUESTIONS YOU MAY WANT TO ASK

When I was job hunting, I always divided my questions into two categories: first some simple ones, to see if I liked the firm and their willingness to answer the questions. Then, if I liked the answers I got to that first set of questions, I would try to dig deeper later or in a follow-up call or letter.

Interviews typically last about 30 minutes, so there are a limited number of questions you can ask. When I was job hunting, there were no company websites I could view, so I had to be creative in finding out about open positions or firm history. Today, because all companies have websites, it is easy to find basic information on a firm before you arrive for your interview. During your interview, asking questions about the way the firm is organized is certainly in order.

I would try to figure out how pigeonholed I might be if I took the job. I always looked for firms organized by team—not task—because I felt with the team approach, there was a better opportunity to pitch in at various times on a project and be able to understand the entire process. Firms that are task-oriented like to have the interns start out helping with projects in the construction documents phase. When you get good at detailing, they keep you there to maximize their efficiency. Unless you ask to be involved in different phases of work, you may be stuck doing CDs for quite a while.

The company's website may give you a hint about their structure, especially if they list their staff with bios and titles. You should look for a structure that enables you to move up.

Asking questions about the types of projects they handle—commercial, residential, housing, medical, educational, etc.—and the percentages of each will help you figure out if they do the type of work you like. Today, it is even possible to figure out a bit about their revenue and, given the number of staff, calculate the revenue per person, providing you with one indication of how a firm is doing.

Asking questions about staff training programs will give you a clue whether the firm desires to keep staff for a longer time or is simply looking to fill a position to get a project out. Firms that hire for projects, and then let staff go after projects are complete, are known in the industry.

Before you leave an interview, make sure you get everyone's business card to get the correct spelling of their names, titles, phone numbers, and email addresses, so you can do proper follow-ups.

FOLLOWING UP

After the interview:

1. Within the next day or so, send a separate email to everyone who was present at the interview.
2. In this follow-up email, thank everyone individually for seeing you. It also gives you a chance to ask someone to clarify some of the points discussed and to ask any additional questions you may have. You can suggest another time to meet to discuss the subjects. That way you show you're hoping for a short negotiation period.
3. If there were some open points or questions they asked that you could not immediately answer, this is the place to do so.

DECIDING AMONG OFFERS

I hope that you will get more than one job offer. Offers usually happen during a meeting, but it could happen in an email or in a follow-up call. *Listen carefully to this advice:* Never say that you have another offer and you will evaluate both offers and get back to them. If you are not prepared to say *yes* or *no* at that moment, say *thank you* and that you will get back to them. *Do not ever play one firm's offer against another.* It will come back to haunt you.

When you receive an offer, it usually means the firm likes you and wants to go the next step, to discuss salary. The offer may also include a base salary figure, but that is just the beginning.

What to Consider before You Accept an Offer

The challenge, from this point, is to figure out how to get all your detailed financial and professional questions answered without annoying anyone. Here are some of the details that you will want to have spelled out to help in making your final decision about which offer to accept:

- If salary was discussed, ask if it is paid biweekly or monthly. Is there automatic deposit at your bank? (If the deposit is made at their bank, you may have to wait a few days before you can move the money into your bank.)
- Is there a year-end bonus? If so, is it based on firm's profitability or on individual performance?
- Do they have formal year-end reviews where they discuss performance *and* compensation?
- Is there a 401K program? If yes, what is the firm's participation?

There are many questions whose answers are included in an employee handbook. Asking to read it may be too forward at this time, but if the subject comes up and you can find a way to ask to see it, it avoids having too many direct questions. Your contact may not even know the correct answers. Here are just a few of those key questions you might want to have answered before you say *yes*:

- What type of medical plan does the firm offer? What is the firm's and the employee's financial participation?
- What is the number of sick days, personal days, and vacation days offered, and can they carry over to the next year?
- Are there times of the year that the firm does not want you to go on vacation?
- Is there life insurance or disability insurance?
- Is there a mileage reimbursement if you use your car for company business? If so, is the amount the federal standard?

- Are personal expense reports submitted monthly? If so, how long before you are reimbursed?
- Can you get an advance when traveling on firm business?
- What will your title be? More important, what are other titles in the office? You may find these on their website in the team list, employee profile section, or career section. Knowing titles will help you determine what you need to know or show to move up the ladder.
- Do they offer training programs you can apply for? If so, are these programs offered during work time or after hours? Does the firm pay for these programs?

Key Points in the Negotiation

1. Understand with whom you are negotiating: Can they make decisions or do they have to go to others for approval?
2. Do not negotiate one item at a time. You will exhaust them. Negotiate multiple points at the same time. Remember, you are looking for a package; let them know what is important to you.
3. Do not rush the negotiation: rushing shows you may be a bit desperate. You want to seem confident—not brash. There are points in all negotiations that are easier for a firm to give up.

 There is a lot to think about before saying, "Yes, I will take the job." If possible, take your time because you will not get a second chance to negotiate the deal.

Most important: get all the final details of a job offer in writing, even if you have to draft the acceptance letter and job description yourself.

HOW TO HANDLE A *NO*

If you get a *no*, you should write a thank-you note to each person you met, thanking them for the interview and the opportunity to discuss the job opening. There are two things you should also keep in mind:

- If this firm was one you were interested in, then add a sentence or two about the fact that you were very impressed with them and hope they keep your résumé on file.

- If they said you were simply not qualified for that particular position, you can say you would be interested in interviewing for another position, because you really liked the firm, the quality of their work, and the people you met.

In Part I, I outlined the most important things you should do to make sure your graduation is remembered as the *start* of a successful career not the *end* of your 5- or 6-year architectural education.

I am sure your last few years will be a grind, as were mine, culminating in a sprint to finish and present your thesis project. *After graduation, the last thing you will want to think about is another "project"—finding a job. That is why preplanning your career is beneficial.*

I am sure none of your professors said, "You need to love the administrative tasks" in the architectural or interior business.

You were taught to love design, not marketing, preparing proposals and making presentations, billing and accounting, HR and office management. By default, many must believe the necessary tasks of programming, budgeting, scheduling, and writing minutes of meetings are unavoidable, distracting from valuable design time.

These administrative and nondesign tasks should be approached as creatively as the design process. You may not like to do these tasks, but they represent, in the real world, about 80 percent of the hours spent on a project. My experience has shown that only about 20 percent of all hours on a project are attributable to design. This book focuses on the 80 percent of the time and the tasks associated with project management and office management.

Graduation should be your springboard to a wonderful career. When you start planning early and break the to-do tasks into small, manageable parts, you can get them done well ahead of graduation and hopefully have a job lined up that you can jump into—after a well-deserved vacation.

I worked every summer, beginning at age 12, at first saving for the fun things I wanted to buy, then during college years to pay for my school expenses. Dad taught me many lessons about getting jobs. Among them:

- Start looking before school was out—beat the crowd
- Preparing a short note why I was interested in working at their company
- Dress appropriately for the interview
- Always send a thank-you note after each interview

I was fortunate to have had three unbelievable summer jobs before college. They all involved steel and construction.

- At 13, I got a job in a steel yard working as a crane operator loading framing angles, reinforcing bars and rolls of mesh onto flatbed trucks. Lesson learned—Pace Yourself. At first, the drivers hated me because I worked too fast.
- At 14, I was moved up to be a driver, on an old pickup that no one else would drive, and delivered steel to construction sites. By the end of the summer, they moved me up to a 20-foot bobtail. I was a little kid and learned quickly that making a delivery mistake was painful. If I made a mistake, I had to get the steel back on the truck by myself. I learned to go slow and read the order two times.
- At 16, I asked to be moved up to driving a tractor trailer, and they agreed. I was in "pig heaven." It was a huge responsibility, loads of fun stopping by at Mom's house for lunch.

PART II

Starting and Excelling at Your Job

CHAPTER 4

Making the Best Impression

DO NOT COME IN LIKE A "BULL IN A CHINA SHOP"

It is natural to be nervous when you join a new firm. Everyone is probably trying to guess your salary and understand your capabilities. They would love to know if you were hired for a new position or to fill an opening. Remember, people are nosy.

I tell all new hires: when you come, be reserved, be respectful, and seem interested in everything that is happening.

Resist the temptation to jump in and be everyone's best friend. Instead, take your time to understand the working relationships at the company you have joined. See who management goes to when they need help, and understand the pecking order. Understand who does what on various projects. You can sometimes find out more just by watching and listening than you can by asking questions.

Lunchtime is often the best way to get a better understanding of the office dynamics. Some bring their lunch, some go out and pick up lunch, some go out to eat, and others go out with clients or their bosses. See how levels mix and find your way slowly. If the office has "lunch and learn" workshops, by all means attend all that you can. You will quickly figure out who the leaders are—they will be the ones asking questions.

If there are vendors who come in for after-work product seminars, go to all the events that you can. Many of these are for AIA credit, and the architects usually attend. as it is a positive way to keep up their credits.

WHAT GOES AROUND COMES AROUND

Whenever a new employee joins our firm, the first thing we talk about is the way we communicate. We go over how we communicate internally with others and how we treat our friends, clients, consultants, and vendors. All of those communications say an enormous amount about who we are both as a company and as individuals. I will be repeating this concept again in the next chapter ("Taking the Plunge") because it is that important.

I can't state enough the significance of treating each person you deal with in the same positive way that you would like to be treated.

It sounds corny, but I for one am very concerned that the sloppy nature of communications can, unfortunately, lead to undesirable results.

I remember when we used to meet in person with clients to confirm ideas, project status, or schedules, or to clear up misunderstandings. We would follow up with letters that we took the time to write with a subject, opening, middle, and closing statement. I know I might sound old-fashioned, but I have too often seen sloppy emails that lead to very embarrassing situations and even litigation. You guessed right; I hate emails as the primary way to communicate. But I know that for so many today, that is the case. So if you're going to rely on emails, at least make sure your emails are well written and that each one has the tone that you are trying to convey.

Everyone should also keep in mind that any email you send may end up projected on a screen in the courtroom. Because of that reality, think twice before you send an email.

There are many other types of communications to consider:

1. **Calls to the office**—For many, calling our office is their first introduction to the firm. Despite the higher costs, we find it very cost-effective to have all calls answered by an extremely knowledgeable person. I admit that we have never tried the alternative of having an automated assistant, but my experience of calling many organizations with the automated assistants is dreadful. I have always wanted to have each staff member answer the phone for an hour or so every once in a while, to understand firsthand just how important the position is. Clients, friends, and vendors can reach each of us directly through direct inward dialing or by calling our cell phones. This has reduced the number of calls to those asking for general information, potential clients looking for one of the principals, vendors asking for appointments to show their products, or others working with us on projects. Each call is always extremely important. I am sure we will never eliminate the opportunity to personally answer each call.

2. **Rewarding good feedback**—We started a policy 35 years ago that if a client told me or one of the other senior folks something nice about a staff member, that staff member would get $50. In our 35 years, we have handed out hundreds of $50 checks. The employees love it, and when the people saying nice things learn of our policy, they are impressed. It works at all levels; however, like most programs, it is not fair for all. Those who do not deal directly with clients do not have the same opportunity for direct praise, so we have alternative policies that recognize such individuals' achievements.

3. **Saying thank you**—Of course some people say "thank you" today, but there should be a lot more people saying it. At our office, we have even gone so far as having thank-you cards printed up so we could send quick notes out to people who did nice things for us. We have sent out hundreds of these cards, and the response is overwhelming.

   In the architectural business, there are so many people we can thank who regularly help us in many ways: manufacturer's reps, product vendors, consultants, and clients who pay on time or early. Each of these groups does a tremendous amount for the firm, and many times they really save us by getting critical information or samples to us for presentations, for example. We must always thank these folks.

4. **Contractual matters**—I tell our folks that all contractual changes should be documented in letter form, not with email communications. Today, if you send a letter, people tend to pay attention, mainly because no one sends a letter anymore. Letters are special, like faxes and FedEx used to be. If you want to make sure it was received, send it "return receipt requested." Contractual issues regarding budget and schedule come up frequently, and it is often important to get your input on the record. If there is a project manager or owner's rep working for the client, it is a good idea to send them both a letter. If you think the issues are important enough and could lead to litigation down the road, I recommend you BCC your professional liability representative at the same time.

5. **Internal communications**—How many times have you seen one employee email another even though that employee is

sitting only a few desks away? If you are scheduling a meeting, then an email is OK, but if you are asking a question, we all know one email will never be enough. So next time you are tempted to ask a question in an email to an employee who's nearby, pick up the phone and call, or try going over to the person and asking the question in person instead.

6. **Helping out your coworker**—Taking the time to help co-workers pays off handsomely. I am not suggesting you do things for the reward—the payoff can be as simple as you have someone to go to when you have a question. First, it helps you understand the kinds of subjects that people may need extra training with, and second, if you are not yet in a management position, it shows that you are a leader, and it may even help you get a raise.

FINDING YOUR NICHE

No matter how many questions you ask in the interview process, the only way you will find out how a firm operates is by joining it.

It is important to meet as many staff members as possible in the interview process to understand the lay of the land and to find out who does what. You will very quickly find out where you stand in the hierarchy and what you need to know and do to move up the project ladder.

"PROJECT-BASED" FIRMS VS. "TASK-BASED" FIRMS

Firms that are "project based" are, in my opinion, much more fun and interesting to work for, because you get to learn how the firm runs a project from start to finish from the client's point of view. Even if the tasks you do from project to project are similar, when you are just beginning in the business, the opportunity to work through all the phases is important. You will find this type of structure mostly in smaller firms. When you are in this situation, ask if you can read the contract, understand the phases and scope to be provided, and learn about all the forms that the firm uses for each phase of work.

On the other hand, if the firm is "task based," organized with groups of project managers, designers, production, furniture, and construction adminis-trators, you will have to work a lot harder to understand how the entire process works. Again, ask if you can read the contract and see the scheduling, cost, personnel and space, minutes of meetings, and punch list forms. Even though you may be working on a single task, most often construction documents when you start, asking will show you are interested in all the phases of the project.

GO FOR THE EXTRA CREDIT

Most offices invite vendors in to present new products or services. These get-togethers usually happen at lunchtime or after work and are designed primarily for the registered architects to keep up their accreditation; they get points for attending.

I recommend trying to attend every extra-credit seminar to understand the subjects the company thinks are important for the staff to know. In addition, you will quickly figure out who are the ones who ask the questions and are the most interested in acquiring additional knowledge.

BEING A DISRUPTOR

What do I mean by "disruptor"? I think of a person or a company as a disruptor when they challenge traditional ways of thinking. You might say that sounds a lot like an innovator, and you would be correct. The two words, disruptor and innovator, are very similar. Google defines disruptors as innovators but says not all innovators are disruptors—in the same way that a square is a rectangle but not all rectangles are squares.

Harvard Business School professor and disruption guru Clayton Christensen says, "Disruption takes a left turn by literally uprooting and changing how we think, behave, do business, learn and go about our day-to-day. A disruption displaces an existing market, industry, or technology and produces something new and more efficient and worthwhile."

I would have loved to be a disruptor, but I will easily settle for being an innovator. In business, I always felt that if you do not take risks, you will never grow, and if you always play by the rules, you will be boring. I try not to play by established rules. Being "disruptive" (which can also mean innovative, ingenious, and original) is fast becoming the new buzzword in American business.

Google, Amazon, Uber, and many other digital companies who started from a clean slate are referred to as disruptors. They are already established—

increasing customer expectations every day. We have all seen how these companies transform their organizations to deliver new, remarkable, adaptable
customer experiences.

Based on my definition, individuals can also be disruptors. Bill Gates, Steve
Jobs, Jeff Bezos, and certainly Elon Musk are described as disruptors. I would
settle for just a few in my firm being just innovators.

Every day things come up in an office where extra effort or new thinking
is required. I have been in many offices where problems are discussed and,
unless the boss asks someone directly to look for a fix or assigns the task to
someone, nothing happens. You should *volunteer.* I call the person willing to
make the extra effort a disruptor—one who disrupts the normal behavior in an
office. We have all heard of the 80/20 rule: that 80 percent of your results will
come from 20 percent of your people. While it is not normal that 20 percent of
the staff volunteer for special projects, even a couple of well-intentioned staff
members with new ideas go a long way.

Every office has a number of improvements that can and should be made.
Management always welcomes extra effort.

Internal Project Processes: Streamlining the Work Sequence to Minimize Churn

"Churn" is what happens after plans are approved and then changed, requiring
time to replan, redesign, and/or represent new ideas. By storyboarding tasks prior
to design, changes can be minimized, saving time for both the firm and the client.

A number of years ago, I brought in a consultant, CONNSTEP, to evaluate
our internal workflow processes. We wanted to determine steps we could either modify or eliminate to improve our delivery system. This type of study is
usually difficult to accomplish with internal staff but quite easy to do when you
bring in a consultant.

CONNSTEP's primary business model was helping Connecticut manufacturers review their processes in order to take on more business without adding
more staff. Our need was similar. Exceptional architectural and interior design
talent is hard to find in any city, and in order to take on more business with the
same number of staff, we also needed to be more efficient. The architectural
business is also a manufacturer—architects manufacture a set of plans used
to build an architectural project.

We asked eight of our staff to participate with CONNSTEP for an hour
each week. We spent time diagramming *all* the steps that happen in a typical

project. We thought we knew every step, yet when we actually created the flow chart with all the variations and possibilities, we were surprised.

We identified five places in the process where churn most frequently happened. By drawing this chart, we could immediately see a pattern of steps that lead to churn.

Problems arose when we:

- Started work prior to the entire consulting team being on board and didn't have the benefit of their initial input
- Started test fits and building evaluation before the envisioning and programming phase was complete with the client
- Started work without a defined budget or at least a budget range to work toward
- Skipped steps due to a schedule change—thinking we would go back and pick up the changes later
- Did not execute handoffs *perfectly* from DD to CD.

By being specific in the way we start each phase, we have eliminated the problem points, saved considerable time and money, and found we have a much easier time meeting the demanding schedules.

Forms

Forms used both internally and externally can always be improved. The need for specific information is constantly changing, and the software we use to prepare the forms is continually improving. Unless we take the time to revisit the purpose of each form, we miss the opportunity to not only provide more value for our clients, but also to save time. Form design is often backward. Most forms are designed to include information the creator needs; we should *first* consider the information the client needs and design the form from that point of view.

The second part of the process is how we deliver the form or information to the client. Is it just emailed, or is it part of a system that organizes the information for easy retrieval? All information should be delivered cloud-based, not in an email, and in a format for easy future access and backup.

Services

Adding new services, especially subscription services, goes a long way to smooth the revenue curve and add to a company's bottom line. Many of the more traditional architectural and interior design firms find services they have always provided now being performed by other members of the project team—the owner's reps, realtors, project managers, furniture dealers, AV and IT consultants, engineers, move/location consultants, and workplace strategy consultants. There is a desperate need to maintain the services you have as well as develop new services to just stay the course.

Go to the websites of the other team members; you will be amazed at how many of your services are provided by multiple firms. Firms with the deepest pockets or firms that use certain services as throwaway or marketing services can quickly compromise the effectiveness of the architects' services. You will find that the similar services others choose to provide have no liability or risk associated with them.

ENTREPRENEUR VS. INTRAPRENEUR

I think we all know the definition of an entrepreneur. In the context of this book, it is a person who strikes out on his or her own to start a new firm. An entrepreneur is the one who, through his or her skills and passion, creates a business and is willing to take full accountability for its success or failure.

I think of all others in two categories:

- Intrapreneurs
- Employees

An "intrapreneur" is someone who utilizes his or her skill, passion, and innovation to manage or create something useful *for someone else's business* . . . with an entrepreneurial zest. Though both are visionaries, the entrepreneur usually spots an opportunity in the marketplace and has the courage and zeal to turn the opportunity into a business. In contrast, the intrapreneur uses his or her passion, drive, and skills to manage the business or create something new and useful for the business.

Another difference between an entrepreneur and an intrapreneur is that an entrepreneur has the freedom to act on his or her whim whereas an intrapreneur may need to ask for management's approval to make certain changes in the company's processes, product design, or any other innovation he or she wants to implement.

Employees are obviously also valuable and are there to support the business. Not everyone can or wants to be an intrapreneur.

Every firm needs all three types:

- The entrepreneur, who has the vision and hopefully sees the opportunity clearly
- The intrapreneur, without whose support and creative thinking success may be more difficult
- The loyal and talented employee whose dedicated efforts produce quality work for the clients

MENTORING

Every office should set up a mentoring program for each employee to have co-workers to bounce ideas off of, check their work, and learn new technical tricks.

The role of the mentor is to guide and support, to be a friend and confidant, and to be a source of information. The need for a mentor will diminish as time goes by and will disappear completely as the new staff member develops his or her own networks of friends and contacts.

Mentors need to be readily accessible and prepared to offer help as the need arises. Mentoring is the best and fastest way for staff to grow. Part of the mentoring program is to have staff read the contracts for the projects they are working on and read all project correspondence and documentation to understand the scope of work, timing, and compensation.

> Project staff should be included on all client correspondence, even if a BCC (blind carbon copy), and when appropriate should attend client meetings and presentations.

Remember, mentoring is a two-way street. Think about what you can do to help others. Perhaps you are great at Photoshop, using Revit, Sketchup, or even basics such as Excel. Ask management if you can lead a "lunch and learn" to help others.

PLANNING FOR THE ARCHITECT REGISTRATION EXAM

My recommendation is to start planning for the exam the day after graduation or the day you start working. Depending on the state where you live, the requirements may be a little different; know the facts about apprenticeship.

A good starting point is to understand the Architectural Experience Program (AXP) fully described at www. NCARB.org. There are extensive resources that will help you understand the experience requirements, how to get started, how to stay active, and all about mentoring.

When you have spent five or six years and a lot of money getting your architectural degree, do not waste a minute thinking you can do this later. Having your license can dramatically change your position and salary in the firm. Having your license will also be very important to the firm from a number of points of view. Here are just three ways that your company benefits from you having your license:

1. The firm can give you a new title and bill you out at a higher rate. (If that is the case, do not forget to ask for a raise.)
2. Having more licensed/registered architects on the company roster looks better for the firm when a potential client is looking at the company's website.
3. Requests for Proposal (RFPs) often ask the question, "How many licensed/registered architects are in the firm and will be assigned to the project?"

With a license, you are *much more marketable.*

Many firms will pay for the courses you take, the course materials you need, and the costs to take the exam and will give you time off with pay to study. This can amount to a sizeable amount of money and time, so keep this in mind as a point of negotiation when you are considering joining a firm.

Get the exam out of the way as fast as you can.

Create a Study Plan

There are a number of ways to create your plan of attack to pass all the tests. The most common approach is to:

- obtain the reference books
- read all the information at NCARB.org

- do independent study
- take the available courses designed to help you understand the subject material in each exam
- study with a friend or friends in your same position

CHAPTER 5

Building Your Reputation

PERSONAL MARKETING

Marketing is certainly the lifeblood of all firms; without any type of marketing, firms would have a very difficult time getting new projects.

Most of what we read about architectural marketing has to do with the types of marketing the firm can do to bring in new business. In this chapter, I explore the types of marketing the individual can do to build their personal reputation and, by doing so, directly assist the firm with overall marketing. Employees are always the firm's best marketers. It is most interesting that employees do not understand how their considerable project efforts translate directly to positive firm marketing.

In our firm, approximately 80 percent of the new projects each year come from past clients. This high percentage is the result of the exceptional work of each of the employees working on those projects.

There are a number of employee myths about marketing:

1. Only principals do marketing.
2. I do not see clients or go to pitches, so I don't need to care about marketing.
3. The firm has not taught me to market, so I do not need to learn to do it.

When a firm has a high percentage of repeat business, the employees should be congratulated for their marketing skills. They probably do not understand that they are marketers. One of the first, and perhaps most important, skills an employee needs to learn about personal marketing is how to deliver the "one-minute elevator pitch." Some firms work with employees practicing pitches because they understand how important the presentation is to the individual hearing it.

When we are with friends who know what business we are in, a typical question might be "What are you working on?" Learning how to deliver a short, exciting answer is so important. Most of the time, the person asking the question is just being polite. However, when they hear your excitement, they will be pleasantly surprised and glad they asked. Practice what you might want to say!

When we meet a person for the first time, we might be asked a similar question: "What kind of work do you do?" or "Who do you work for?" Both are questions that require fun short answers. Both questions are surprisingly difficult to answer without fumbling a bit. When you can deliver a short, interesting answer, you will be surprised how people will remember you. Practice, practice, practice!

If you are meeting a person who might be a potential client and are asked "What does your firm do?" your answer should be very different from other more personal questions. The way you answer may influence the opportunity for the firm to hear about future work. Practice what you might want to say!

It is natural for people to want to be around people who are excited about what they do, just like clients want to work with firms that are excited about their projects. Enthusiasm is contagious. You might not think you are marketing, but you are—you are doing personal branding and indirect firm marketing.

Can you give a concise answer to those questions in less than a minute? Stop reading here and try it.

A few TV shows have guests describe what they do in a minute or so, and then the participants are judged on their presentations. One minute is a long time. Without talking too fast, you can pack in a lot of information into a minute. However, when you are not organized with your thoughts, a minute might seem like an eternity. If your answer is not exciting, the ability for others to listen and comprehend what you have to say is reduced exponentially. So create and practice your personal elevator pitches.

Whether you want your own firm someday or are professionally satisfied moving up the ladder, it is important to know how to make short, effective pitches. If you are also part of the management team, making pitches for new work is a necessity. What you say in this capacity will of course be less personal and more firm-oriented.

In addition to knowing how to deliver a great elevator pitch, there are a number of other ways to build your personal brand. First, let us explore why you should want to build your personal brand, especially if you do not have your own firm. There are four reasons.

The better you are known in the industry:

1. The higher the salary you can command
2. The easier it will be to change jobs, if desired
3. The more you will be associated with your firm and indirectly be able to help them acquire new business
4. The easier it will be if you ever want to hang up your own shingle

There are a number of easy ways to build your personal brand. You may be doing many of these things already, and with some tweaking you can help both yourself and your firm.

- **Volunteer Work**—Help organizations plan afterwork or weekend programs. These could be as simple as helping to organize walks or runs for a cause. There are organizations that help the less fortunate with home repairs, food banks, clothing banks, and caretaking. Often the firm will sponsor you in these activities. This is good for you as well as the firm. Your personal activities can be supported and included on your company's website, on Facebook, Instagram, Twitter, and other types of social media.
- **Larger-Scale Programs**—Participate in activities with groups such as Habitat for Humanity, Teach for America, Americares, Save the Children, and City Year. There are hundreds of these national programs, plus even more local groups that desperately need help.
- **Education**—Be an adjunct professor at your local community college or university.
- **Civic Boards**—A wonderful way to help the community as well as your firm is to participate on local boards such as architectural review, environmental planning, zoning, the local school board, and economic development. Your specific expertise in planning, design, and construction will be welcome.
- **Local Organizations**—There are organizations like the Rotary, Knights of Columbus, Lions Club, and Kiwanis that have civic-minded activities going all year long.
- **Social Media**—On a more personal level, everyone is involved with Facebook, LinkedIn, Houzz, Snapchat, etc.

- **Speaking Engagements**—Many firms have their clients in for events, and staff will chat about new workplace strategies and project case studies. You can speak at your local AIA, IFMA, or ASID about your specialty.

These are some of the ways you can build your personal brand. In summary, enhancing your personal brand will help you:

- Win more clients for your company to increase sales and increase your earnings
- Land better clients for your company to make your company more efficient
- Grow your professional network so you open more professional opportunities
- Build online communities to further increase professional opportunities
- Lay the foundation for future success, however you define it

WORK RELATIONSHIPS

Getting Along with Coworkers

I wrote an earlier section on "what goes around comes around." This certainly applies to the importance of getting along with coworkers. Most take this comment for granted and believe it is not necessary to write a paragraph about it, but I disagree. There are so many times when interviewing that I ask "How did you hear about us?" and the reply is that a friend, coworker, current employee, or former employee told them about the firm. Most jobs come through referrals, not want ads. It may seem that coworkers are like competitors—for a promotion, raise, or additional responsibility on a project. When this happens, staff members do not watch one another's backs and projects suffer. Strong relationships benefit all. Resist talking about coworkers to others. If you find a mistake in the work of a coworker, go to them directly, never their boss. Embarrassing someone will certainly backfire on you.

Getting Along with Your Boss

I thought about leaving this section out but then thought about a few experiences where employees lost their cool. After those incidents, it is difficult asking the boss for a recommendation. Owners understand that employees move around, especially younger ones trying to decide what they like to do, and most are willing to give a recommendation if asked. It will be hard, or impossible, to ask for a recommendation if you blow up at your boss. Since you want the best recommendation you can get, be mindful of your temper.

Getting along does not mean you should not speak your mind. If you do not understand what you are being asked to do, or you just flatly do not agree with the request, ask for a meeting with your boss to discuss the subject. One thing you should avoid doing is going to a coworker and badmouthing your boss. It will get back to him or her very quickly. Most of the time, the issue you have with your boss will be a misunderstanding or misinterpretation of the task, which can be cleared up quite simply. Clearing the air is very positive. Being proactive, by not letting an issue fester, is also a very productive way to handle problems. If you are being asked to do or draw something you do not agree with, sometimes it is best to do what was asked. You can also do what you think may be a better solution, and then ask for time to discuss both options. You may be overruled, but you will be respected and remembered for trying to help.

Architecture is a creative and innovative profession. You will make a great impression with your boss if you try to create something new. Be innovative. You could recommend improvements to your firm's services or, better yet, think up a new service the firm can offer. Is there a service you can recommend that will be a subscription service, having a scheduled, recurring fee rather than a fixed fee? Services sold on a subscription basis—like your cable TV, music streaming service, or Netflix—level out the highs and lows of the income stream.

Getting Along with Clients, Suppliers, and Vendors

When you are looking for a new job, having references from different sources is very helpful, because each one looks at you and your work life from a unique perspective. Previous employers write mostly about your work experiences and performance at their company; vendors will comment about your professionalism. Always try to develop your professional relationships with suppliers and vendors as well as with clients.

Part II outlined guidelines for basic working etiquette needed to succeed in a professional office environment. Students move quickly from a very structured family environment to a free, rough-and-tumble, unstructured environment in school in a matter of months. After that, interns need to learn a new vocabulary and new ways to communicate with others; they have a newfound freedom requiring discipline to succeed.

Fortunately, the rules one needs to apply when working in an architectural or interior design office are simple and very logical, much like the basics learned while growing up at home.

When you join a firm, you will feel proud of having completed a rigorous five- or six-year program. You will quickly realize, however, that you are the beginner; you should take your time to understand how the office works and listen more than you speak. As you find your place in the group, you can ask questions, learn who does what, and begin to learn the firm's processes and procedures. In time, you can make suggestions and think about mentoring others.

The profession is a small club of individuals you will be with for years. After a short time of being involved in your office and with outside professional organizations, you will know many of the players. These relationships will stay with you for years.

The way you build your reputation with the other employees, vendors, clients, and associates in related businesses is critical to being able to leverage relationships in the future, whether you are looking for a new job or starting your own firm.

PART III

Architecture Is a Team Sport

CHAPTER 6

Managing Handoffs

When you start to feel comfortable about the way you are working, and you feel like your experiences and successes are firing on all cylinders, that is the best time for a business *reset*. Wait too long and you will find your marketing gets stale, employees are not as precise about details, and profit slips. Business practices must be constantly reset to keep the firm fresh and on its best game.

The graphic on the preceding page illustrates the handing off of a baton. The owners of the hands have not quite completed the handoff. That is what I see happening in business today, especially architecture. We are all running as fast as we can but do not seem to be able to complete our work before we need to hand it off to the next group so they can add their valuable information.

Until I started thinking about architecture as a "team sport" in addition to architecture as a business, I missed the subtle adjustments needed to be made to each of the phases of work to make the process smoother, more fulfilling for the employees, and, yes, more profitable for the firm.

Architecture and interior design are very complex businesses. Not only are there many teams involved in even the smallest of projects, there are also many players on each team. Because so many people are involved, the project may be handed off to others many times.

There are a couple of types of handoffs:

1. Internal handoffs—from person to person or group to group within the firm
2. External handoffs—from firm to firm

While both have similar components, internal handoffs are usually taken less seriously yet can have consequences that affect the firm's profitability and timing. With internal handoffs, you are most likely dealing with friends and coworkers; the thought is that, if something is missing in the transfer of information, you can fix the problem very quickly. The reality is just the opposite. Overly casual handoffs may:

- Cause the receiving group delays in finishing their work
- Result in work that needs to be redone, affecting profitability
- Lead to bad feelings between the individual(s) transferring the information and the individual(s) receiving the information

Internal handoffs are often not visible to the outside world, especially to the client, and the financial losses are usually limited to loss of time. These same issues are of course true when external handoffs do not go smoothly.

When one firm does not transfer information smoothly to another, the stakes can often be higher. For instance, the client may get involved if the schedule or budget is impacted; the receiving firm may have additional costs that they will want reimbursed; or there may be a ripple effect if firms need to redo work or cannot meet schedules. Clients will not look kindly to paying extra to a firm for errors caused by another.

There are two prime types of handoff failures:

1. A handoff *is not* made on schedule because the work is not complete
2. A handoff is made on schedule but the work is not complete, with the intent of following up later with the missing detail

Most people think the responsibility for a successful handoff belongs to the one who transfers information to another. This is only half true. The receiving group also has the responsibility to let the sender know what they expect to efficiently do their work.

The graphic of the baton transfer in a relay race perhaps shows it best. The person handing off the baton must be in the right place at the right time—on schedule—with the baton extended in their hand so it can be firmly placed in the hand of the receiver. Similarly, the receiver must take off at precisely the right time, get up to speed, and have their hand extended behind to receive the baton. If both are not moving at the right speed and in the right position, either they will collide or be too far apart to make the handoff. The only way handoffs work perfectly is with a lot of practice.

An internal group, delivering information to another, should make a list of what they will be delivering, and a group receiving information should let the sender know what they expect. Even though we tend to think of these hand-offs as being informal, they need to be monitored to be successful.

These same comments hold true for handoffs to external groups. The basic difference is that the stakes can be more serious when handoffs are between firms. Each of the parties has responsibility for communicating what they expect from the other. Communicating what each group plans to do goes a long way to assuring a successful handoff. Many use a handoff agreement worksheet, which is designed to capture the detail each group needs.

Not only is the group handing off specific information; they are also pass-ing on responsibility. A handoff presumes the client has signed off on a spe-cific body of work. In the initial phase called programming, the client and architect discuss subjects such as the company culture, products and ser-vices, workplace strategies, headcount, operating principles, workflow, growth equipment, and furniture. To move on to the next phase, the architect will produce a report summarizing this information and ask the client to sign off. Only then should the architect move on to conceptual designs. If the architect does not get a sign-off for a phase, then the design work should not start on the next phase.

Changes are expected to happen all the time. Changes in early phases may not have a great impact on budget or schedule, but as the work pro-gresses, changes in scope can have significant implications to the firms and their teams.

These are the major "handoffs" in an architectural/interior design project:

External: Client → Architect → Programming Information*

Internal: Architect → Programming to Test Fit Team

Internal: Architect → Test Fit Team to SD Team

Internal: Architect → SD Team to DD Team

External: Architect → to Structural Engineer

External: Architect → to MEP Engineers

Internal: Architect → Team to CD Team*

External: Architect → CD coordination with all Engineers*

External: Architect → CD coordination with IT, AV, Security*

External: Architect → CD coordination with Furniture Group*

Review of Construction Documents with all Players

External: Architect → CD review with Town Officials*

Internal: Architect → to CM or General Contractor*

These steps are required even for small interior design projects.

*All steps and handoffs of information are important. Those marked with an asterisk (*) represent handoffs of responsibility and should be treated more formally.

Prior to each handoff, there is a considerable amount of information that can be prepared in a worksheet or checklist format. After these worksheets are prepared for a few projects, you will find the list becomes quite valuable and makes things easier to track and manage.

ENVISIONING WITH THE CLIENT: FIRST HANDOFF OF INFORMATION

Whether your client is planning a new building, looking to purchase or lease a building, or simply replanning existing interior space, the first step should always include meetings with senior management and the person(s) assigned to manage the project.

The more face time architects have with senior management and the client's internal project manager, the more successful the project will be. Senior management needs to understand how important their initial input is in setting the course for the project.

The first series of meetings is called *Envisioning Sessions*. This is the expression used in the profession when discussing the client's big-picture plans. These meetings may only take a couple of hours and should include anyone on the client side with direct responsibility for the success of the project.

Always remember to send the client sample questions in advance of the meeting. No one likes to be surprised—especially the boss. Here is a typical set of high-level subjects to discuss with the senior management of your client:

- *Culture*—discuss the company's Mission and Vision statements. Some companies describe their goals in terms of their Vision, Promise, and Values. We try to understand these goals in terms of the employee as well as the customer.
- *Business Overview*—review of existing products and services, planned products and services, and special needs
- *Staffing Overview*—review of historical and projected staff growth by department or function
- *Location Overview*—discussion of need to be in a different location to easily attract employees, have easier employee access, be closer to trains, highways, airports, clients, restaurants, and shopping areas
- *Facility Overview*—need for improved layout to have better workflow and workplace strategy, expansion potential, and employee amenities
- *Environmental Overview*—desire to be in a "green" facility for improved employee health, less absenteeism, and increased productivity
- *Space Overview*—less space may be required due to implementation of hoteling, free addressing, work-at-home programs, and flexible scheduling
- *Lease Overview*—review desired lease features: rental rate bumps, expansion/contraction/cancellation options
- *Budget*—set a total budget with contingencies

Other categories of questions include the company's desired image, age brackets of staff, percentages of men vs. women, and education spread. We ask if there have been any official or unofficial surveys taken about their existing space, including building amenities, furniture, technology, colors, materials, and even subjects such as temperature control systems.

 Asking business questions is fine; asking questions about architectural concepts, unless the client has experience with real estate, planning and design, or construction, should be held for a later time. Remember, unless you have had prior experience with the client, you may not get straight answers to questions about budget or schedule. If you ask what is your budget, human nature is to give a lower number. If you ask what is your schedule, human nature is to give you a shorter time. If you believe the budget may be too little or the timeframe too short, now is the time to have that discussion. You want to be on record with reasons why you differ.

PROGRAMMING: EVALUATE EXISTING CONDITIONS

After the envisioning session and prior to preparing a personnel and space forecast, it is important to understand how the client uses their existing space. An evaluation of the use of the space from an occupancy point of view is a very important exercise. It is necessary to determine how people work today:

- how often their workspace is occupied
- existing private office sizes, shared spaces, open workplace types and sizes, touchdown or visitor spots, etc.
- how and where they communicate with others
- how often they receive visitors
- which departments have heavy conferencing needs
- which departments need access to special technology or storage
- which departments are most likely to expand, stay the same size, or reduce in size
- use of special spaces such as cafeteria, large multipurpose rooms, copy centers, dedicated computer room, mailroom, boardroom, fitness center, pantries, libraries, file rooms, loading dock, and building lobby

Conference rooms are a category unto themselves. Many companies indicate they are always short of conference rooms. After survey, it is often determined the reason for the shortage is that the larger rooms, those that can handle 8–10 people or more, are most often used by about 4 people. Rooms without technology such as AV, IT, conferencing, smart boards, etc., may also be underutilized. This information is valuable when projecting future conferencing needs.

PROGRAMMING: PRELIMINARY STAFF AND SPECIAL USE SPACE NEEDS

After analyzing how the client uses their existing space, the second step is to project preliminary space needs for both people and special support spaces. The usable space number will be used to test the quality of the *fit* of the proposed sites in terms of efficiency and functionality. The improvements required to the base buildings and the interior systems are used to project proposed budgets and schedules.

Moving to a new facility or making significant changes to an existing facility is an opportunity to explore new ways of working. Companies of all sizes are exploring more collaborative work settings affecting numbers of private offices, design of open workstations with either lower or no panels separating work positions, smaller meeting areas for 2–4 persons, and much less filing and storage space. Conference areas are planned with all sorts of technology, and many are open or semiprivate, divided by glass walls or white boards. There is a trend back to more open environments to facilitate collaboration and flexibility. Many companies have even pushed the limit to "one size workplace for all" and "not everyone will automatically have a dedicated workplace."

There are no shortages of consultants assisting corporations in workplace programming and planning. Realtors, owner's reps, project managers, furniture manufacturers and dealers, and certainly architects offer a wide variety of services from conceptual analysis to implementation of design concepts.

Many approach the exercise of workplace strategy from a space utilization point of view focusing on ways to save space and thus reduce costs. If a company's desire is to save real estate costs, the exercise is straightforward and includes reducing the number and size of private offices, reducing the size of workstations by introducing concepts like benching, and introducing a series of alternative work options such as work-at-home programs. These are programs where individuals do not have a dedicated workstation at the main office.

I have always been a proponent of the idea that space is an asset, yet I understand the importance of keeping costs as low as possible. In service-type businesses, staff costs run about 85–92 percent of total expenditures, with real estate costs usually second at around 6 percent. In some businesses, technology costs are gradually moving up to second place, behind staff costs, making my point even more strongly that space be considered an asset.

Other workplace strategists focus on planning opportunities to maximize collaboration through creative planning and design techniques. They focus more on the utilization of space, occupancy analysis, and the evaluation of circulation patterns to determine the best locations for chance meetings. Many have determined that meaningful chance meetings happen most often at a person's workstation—not the café, interconnecting star, or in the lounge as one might imagine. To promote this type of collaboration, workstations should be designed to permit a pull-up bench or chair in such a way as not to visually or acoustically disturb others.

SAMPLE PROGRAM DOCUMENT

The following personnel and space form can be used for projecting both preliminary space needs and final company space requirements, the difference being the amount of departmental workflow information needed for the preparation of design layouts.

The form is designed to enter staff numbers with their corresponding space standards on the left side and special area needs with corresponding space standards on the right side. The form is used as a single page for the preliminary forecast and with multiple pages, one sheet per department, stacked in Excel for the final space report.

Projecting staffing needs over 5- or 10-year occupancy is difficult. Staff represents the major expense stream of the company, and no one is good at projecting their expenses. Staff numbers are always more accurate when management first projects the business and their income stream, then translates business growth to personnel growth by function or department. Most companies have developed personnel/revenue ratios for both line and staff groups. Architects use those numbers in the form and test workplace standards to project space needs.

It is recommended that the initial test fits and final plan and design concepts be based on maximum staffing and maximum special use requirements. It is difficult and expensive to make changes to a plan after a few years of occupancy to accommodate additional growth. This is shown on the following chart:

PERSONNEL AND SPACE PROJECTION FORM

Pg.	Position	Off Type	Exist	Year 2018	Year 2023	Year 2028	Area Std	Dept 2018	Dept 2023	Dept 2028
2	CEO	A	1	1	1	1	400	400	400	400
3	Administrative Asst	E	1	1	1	1	96	96	96	96
4	President	A	1	1	1	1	400	400	400	400
5	Administrative Asst	E	1	1	1	1	96	96	96	96
6							0	0	0	0
7	CFO	B	1	1	1	1	240	240	240	240
8	Administrative Asst	E	1	1	1	1	96	96	96	96
9	VP Finance	C	1	1	1	1	180	180	180	180
10	Director of Finance	E	1	1	1	2	96	96	96	192
11	Accountants	F	4	6	8	10	64	384	512	640
12							0	0	0	0
13	VP Marketing	C	1	1	1	1	180	180	180	180
14	Administrative Asst	E	1	1	1	1	96	96	96	96
15	Analysts	F	3	6	7	9	64	384	448	576
16	Product Leaders	E	2	4	6	8	96	384	576	768
17							0	0	0	0
18	VP Real Estate	C	1	1	1	1	180	180	180	180
19	Administrative Asst	E	1	1	1	1	96	96	96	96
20	Leasing Coordinators	E	1	1	3	5	96	96	288	480
21	Lease Administration	F	1	1	1	3	64	64	64	192
22							0	0	0	0
23	VP Planning and Design	C	1	1	1	1	180	180	180	180
24	Sr. Project Manager	E	1	1	1	2	96	96	96	192
25	Project Managers	F	1	2	3	5	64	128	192	320
26	Designers	F	1	3	5	7	64	192	320	448
27							0	0	0	0
28	VP IT	C	1	1	1	1	180	180	180	180
29	Sr. Programmer	E	1	3	5	8	96	288	480	768
30	Programmers	F	1	3	5	7	64	192	320	448
31	Consultants	I	1	1	1	3	252	252	252	756
32	Receptionist		1	1	1	1	0	0	0	0
33										
	Total Staff		30	46	60	83	Sub-Total	4,976	6,064	8,200

Special Use

Special Use	Exist	Year 2018	Year 2023	Year 2028	Area Std	Space 2018	Space 2023	Space 2028
Board Room - Seating 16	1	1	1	1	600	600	600	600
Ante Room		1	1	1	200	200	200	200
Private Toilet		1	1	1	64	64	64	64
Pantry	1	1	1	1	100	100	100	100
						0	0	0
Conference Rm - 6-8	1	1	1	3	225	675	675	675
Conference Rm - 10-12	1	1	1	1	400	400	400	400
						0	0	0
Lunchroom	1	1	1	1	300	300	300	300
Copy Rooms	1	3	3	3	150	450	450	450
Receiving Area		1	1	1	200	200	200	200
File Room / Fireproof		1	1	1	150	150	150	150
Library		1	1	1	150	150	150	150
Server Room	1	1	1	1	250	250	250	250
						0	0	0
Satellite Pantry	1	1	1	1	64	64	64	64
Visitor Coats	0	0	0	0	0.66	0	0	0
Staff Coats		46	60	83	0.66	30	40	55
Department Total - Special Use						3,633	3,643	3,658

	2018	2023	2028
Special Use	3,633	3,643	3,658
Circulation 40%	3,444	3,883	4,743
Total Usable Area	12,053	13,589	16,601
Estimated Rentable Area 25%	16,071	18,119	22,135
USF / Person	262	226	200

Preferred Adjacencies:

LOCATION-BUILDING-SITE COMPARISON CHECKLIST

Based on preliminary space forecasts, location criteria, and quality guidelines, the realtor will identify a number of buildings for the team's review. The list is narrowed down as the team studies each location.

It is important to create a Building Comparison Checklist to document the features of each building. The decision as to which building makes the cut varies according to the factors most important to the client.

This building comparison form works well:

Building Comparison Checklist

		Building 1	Building 2
	Project Site:		
	Prepared By:		
	Date Prepared / Updated:		
A	**Building Contact Information**		
1	Contact Name		
2	Facility Location		
3	Address		
4	City/State/Zip Code		
5	Building Office Phone Number		
6	Building Office Fax Number		
7	Alternate Phone Number		
8	Building Contact Person		
B	**Building Leasing Agent**		
1	Company/Contact		
2	Address		
3	City/State/Zip Code		
4	Office Phone Number		
5	Office Fax Number		
6	Alternate Phone Number		
7	Contact Person		
C	**Site Characteristics**		
1	Quality of Surrounding Neighborhood		
2	Total Ease of Access to Site		
3	Major Airport (Distance in Minutes)		
4	Train Station (Distance in Minutes)		
5	Bus Stop (Distance in Minutes)		
6	Highway Access (Distance in Minutes)		
7	Loading Dock Availability		
8	Parking Availibility (Including Surrounding Area)		
9	On-site parking available(per 1000 RSF)		
10	Is on-site parking assigned?		
11	Is off-site parking available?		

		Building 1	Building 2
D	**Building Physical Characteristics**		
1	General Building Assessment		
2	Building Age (Years)		
3	Building Construction Type		
4	Floor Slab Construction Type		
5	Floor Live-Load Capacity (lbs./s.f.)		
6	Exterior Wall Construction		
7	Operable Windows		
8	Number of Elevators Cars (Passenger)		
9	Number of Elevators Cars (Freight)		
10	Meets Accessibility Requirements		
11	Building Infrastructure Assessment		
12	HVAC Distribution System Type (Base Bldg.)		
13	Is supplemental HVAC permissible?		
14	Is after hours HVAC available?		
15	Available Watts per RSF per Floor		
16	Is Standby Power available for use?		
17	Standby Power Type Available for Use		
18	Generator Capacity Available for Use (kW)		
19	Is a generator permitted?		
20	Is building fully sprinkled?		
21	Is there an automatic Fire Alarm System?		
22	Is there an automatic Smoke Detection System?		
23	Is there a compatible Access Control System?		
24	Growth Potential		
25	Total Number of Floors		
26	Building Gross Area - 'GA'		
27	Total Building Rentable Area - 'TRA'		
28	Total Building Usable Area - 'TUA'		
29	Building Area Efficiency Factor (TUA/TRA)		
E	**Premises Characteristics**		
1	Premises Compatibility to Client Requirements		
2	Number of Floors Required		
3	Which Floors are Proposed for Occupancy?		
4	Are Floors Contiguous?		
5	Total Usable Area Required		
6	Total Rentable Area Required		
7	Total Percent of Building Occupied by Client		
8	Area Calculation Standard		
9	Existing Condition of Space		
10	Extent of Tenant Fit-up Required		
F	**Lease Terms**		
1	Lease Terms Compatibility to Client Requirements		
2	Start Date		
3	End Date		
4	Can Occupancy Date be Met?		
5	Term (Months)		
6	Type of Lease (Net/Gross)		
7	Renewal Option Available		
8	Expansion Option Available		
9	Rental Rate at Commencement ($/RSF)		
10	Free Rent Period (months)		
11	T.I. Allowance / RSF		
12	Utility Rate / RSF		
13	Restoration Required		

AREA ANALYSIS

Architects are often asked to measure space to confirm the building owner's space representation. For buildings, where the owner uses the Building and Owners Management Association (BOMA) method for calculation, it is easy for the architect to verify the usable and rentable of a building or piece of space.

Buildings are measured several ways. Using the BOMA-measured definition, the total *rentable square feet* (RSF) equals the gross floor area minus all the holes in the floor, such as vertical penetrations, stairways, elevator shafts, large mechanical shafts, upper part of double-height spaces, and so forth. Using the BOMA method, the total rentable square feet is always less than the gross building area.

In the 1980s, building owners in larger cities like New York City began using a new method of measurement called REBNY, after its promoter, the Real Estate Board of New York. Using this method for calculating space, there is no way an architect can verify the owner's RSF numbers because REBNY is not a definite method of measurement. The method allows each owner to apply their own discretionary "market loss factor" to the calculation of usable square feet (USF). USF in REBNY is also different from USF in BOMA, again confusing the comparison. Using the REBNY method, the total RSF is always greater than the gross building area. For owners who say they "measure" according to REBNY, the only way an architect can compare building efficiencies is to calculate and compare the usable (carpetable) area of each building.

Note on the following charts the total building RSF using the REBNY method of measurement is 5,883 SF larger than using the BOMA method of measurement. Is anyone surprised that landlords and building owners prefer the REBNY method of measurement?

Understanding the detail of the two methods is not as important as knowing that comparisons of spaces in two or more buildings can *only* be made by measuring tenants' (carpetable) area as a percentage of the owners' RSF.

The following charts compare the two methods of measurement for the same building.

TEST FITS

Test fits for architectural or interior projects are required to determine how well a property or space functions for a specific client purpose. These concept drawings are often done quickly; however, the plan needs to be sufficiently de-

BOMA - Building Area Analysis

Floor	Gross Area	Core Deduct*	Building Common Area to Apportion	Net RSF per Floor	Net RSF % of Total	Building Area to Apportion to Floor	Total RSF per Floor	Floor Common Area Deduct*	Total USF per Floor	Floor Area Loss Factor Deduct*	Tenant Name	USF per Tenant	RSF per Tenant	RSF % of Total
	Measured	Measured	Measured	C-(D+E)	F/Tot RSF	G X E	F + H	Measured	F - J	1 - (K / I)		Calculated	Calculated	% Of Tot RSF
Basement	4,900	443	399	4,058	20.47%	99	4,157		4,058	2.38%		4,058	4,157	20.47%
First Floor	5,100	631	85	4,384	22.12%	107	4,491		4,384	2.38%		4,384	4,491	22.12%
Second Floor	7,575	525		7,050	35.57%	172	7,222	575	6,475	10.35%		6,475	7,222	35.57%
Third Floor	4,209	180		4,029	20.33%	98	4,127	135	3,894	5.65%		3,894	4,127	20.33%
Penthouse	300			300	1.51%	7	307		300	2.38%		300	307	1.51%
TOTALS:	22,084	1,779	484	19,821	100.00%	484	20,305	710	19,111	5.88%		19,111	20,305	100.00%

*CORE DEDUCTIONS: Elevator and stair shafts and vertical penetrations such as duct shafts, atriums or double-height spaces, etc.

*COMMON FLOOR DEDUCTIONS: Remaining core areas including toilets, elevator lobby, tele/elec and janitor closets, etc.

*Calculations prepared based upon single-tenant occupancy for each floor

REBNY - Real Estate Board Of NY

Floor	Gross Area	Vertical Shafts*		Total USF per Floor	REBNY Loss Factor 25%	RSF Per Floor	Tenant Name	USF per Tenant	RSF per Tenant	RSF % of Total Gross Area
	Measured	Measured	Measured	C-(D+E)	F - J	1 - (K / I)		Calculated	Calculated	% Of Tot RSF
Basement	4,900	443		4,457	5,411	5,411		4,457	5,411	110.42%
First Floor	5,100	631		4,469	5,845	5,845		4,469	5,845	114.61%
Second Floor	7,575	525		7,050	9,400	9,400		7,050	9,400	124.09%
Third Floor	4,209	180		4,029	5,372	5,372		4,029	5,372	127.63%
Penthouse	300	180		120	160	160		120	160	53.33%
TOTALS:	22,084	1,959		20,125	26,188	26,188		20,125	26,188	118.58%

*Vertical Shafts: Elevator and stair shafts and vertical penetrations such as duct shafts, atriums or double-height spaces, etc.

*Calculations prepared based upon single-tenant occupancy for each floor

tailed so that if a building is selected, it will work for the client. As I note in the next two sections, even if the test fit works well, both the budget and schedule need to be evaluated to make sure costs of the required scope will not exceed the budget, and/or the schedule for the work can be met.

SETTING AN ACHIEVABLE SCHEDULE

The time for the team to do its work may vary for each building, depending upon the condition of the existing space, the proposed scope, the permits required, and the client's availability to work with the team in evaluating options. It is important that the architect prepare a separate schedule for each property. The overall schedule may be one of the determining factors in the selection of a building. Similar to programming, preparing a schedule is a two-step process. The first step is a very simple schedule to determine duration of major tasks. The second, more detailed schedule is prepared after a building is selected. When preparing a detailed schedule, it is beneficial to be able to sort the data several ways in order to produce:

- A schedule listing all of the consultants' tasks in the order they will be done, *or*
- A schedule listing the client tasks, in the order you need the client to be available

 Schedules produced to please clients, showing they can move in or relocate by an unrealistic date, always lead to trouble. Most frequent missteps are when sufficient time is not allocated to:

- Find properties, negotiate the deal, and complete the purchase or lease documentation
- Test each of the location options in enough detail to be sure the preliminary budgets and schedules are appropriate
- Enable the building owners sufficient time to complete their work, if applicable
- Enable clients to have adequate time to review, modify, or approve the various presentations
- Submit plans to local and governmental agencies for review and permits

Simple Schedule - Building 1

Task	Jan	Feb	Mar	Apr	May	Jun	Jul	Aug	Sep	Oct	Nov	Dec
Site Selection	▬	▬										
Lease Negotiation		▬	▬									
Test Fits		▬	▬									
Schematic Design			▬	▬								
Design Development				▬	▬							
Construction Docs					▬	▬						
Construction							▬	▬	▬	▬		
Punch List										▬	▬	
Move-In												▬

Simple Schedule - Building 2

Task	Jan	Feb	Mar	Apr	May	Jun	Jul	Aug	Sep	Oct	Nov	Dec
Site Selection	▬	▬										
Lease Negotiation		▬	▬									
Test Fits		▬	▬									
Schematic Design			▬	▬								
Design Development				▬	▬							
Construction Docs					▬	▬						
Construction						▬	▬	▬				
Punch List							▬	▬				
Move-In									▬			

Simple Schedule - Building 3

Task	Jan	Feb	Mar	Apr	May	Jun	Jul	Aug	Sep	Oct	Nov	Dec
Site Selection	▬	▬										
Lease Negotiation		▬	▬									
Test Fits		▬	▬									
Schematic Design			▬	▬								
Design Development				▬	▬							
Construction Docs					▬	▬						
Construction							▬	▬	▬			
Punch List									▬	▬		
Move-In										▬		

Note: Relocating to Building 2 gets the tenant in the earliest.

PREPARING AN APPROPRIATE BUDGET

Similarly, the proposed cost estimate for each option may be a determining factor in selecting a building. The budget format we use for testing locations is the same as the detailed form for budget control through all phases. It takes into account all costs on the left side including demo work, base building work above standard allowance, full tenant scope of work, landlords' contribution, and all other consultants' costs including furniture, AV, IT, moving, security, branding, and so forth.

It is important to use the same format though all phases so the client gets used to seeing a "total project budget." Even though the team may not be responsible for budgets, tracked in various departmental databases, having the information on one form is positive. The four budget categories most difficult to nail down in the early phases are:

- Security
- IT equipment, power and generator
- Audiovisual
- Furniture

Individual numbers will change as there is more detail about location and design, but at least each stakeholder is on notice that they need to be responsible for their work.

Staying within the client's approved "Corporate AR" (appropriation request) is mandatory if you want a happy client and repeat business. The first budget example shows how to track preliminary budgets where three buildings are under consideration. The second budget example (notice the left side categories are the same) shows how columns are added to include the Schematic Design (SD), Design Development (DD), and Final Costs numbers. This is one of the most important forms the client reviews throughout the project. All contractors and consultants should be asked to present their figures in this format.

The Pre-Lease Budget for a three-building comparison is followed by the more detailed format showing Pre-Lease, SD, DD, Approved and Final Costs all on one form. Both contain the same categories of costs.

Preliminary Project Budget Form

	Expense Category	Description	Building A	Building B	Building C
A	**Base Interior Fit-Up**				
1	Demolition				
2	Rough Carpentry				
3	Drywall				
4	Ceiling				
5	Millwork				
6	Glass/Mirror				
7	Hollow Metal				
8	Doors, Frames, and Hardware				
9	HVAC				
10	Plumbing				
11	Sprinkler				
12	Lighting				
13	Electrical/Fire Alarm				
14	Flooring-yds.				
15	Wall Finishes				
16	Specialties				
17	IT Network and Cable Mgmt				
B	**Above Standard TI**				
1	Communicating Stair				
2	Fitness Center/Toilets/Locker Rms				
3	Cafeteria, etc.				
4	Floor Reinforcing				
5	Computer Room (based on sq. ft.)				
C	**Base Building Upgrades**				
1	Restrooms				
2	Main & Parkng Lobbies				
3	Elevators				
		Sub-Total Construction Costs	$0	$0	$0
		Construction Contigency	$0	$0	$0
		General Conditions	$0	$0	$0
		CM Fee	$0	$0	$0
		Insurance	$0	$0	$0
		Sales Tax on CM Services	$0	$0	$0
		Building Permit	$0	$0	$0
		Sub-Total CM Related Fees	$0.00	$0.00	$0.00
		Projected Construction Costs	$0.00	$0.00	$0.00
		Less Value of Landlord Contribution			
		Net (after allowance) Construction Costs	$0.00	$0.00	$0.00
D	**Consultant Fees**				
1	Architect/Interior Design				
2	Owner's Rep/PM				
3	MEP Engineer				
4	Structural Engineer				
5	Lighting Consultant				
6	Acoustical Consultant				
7	AV Consultant				
8	IT Consultant				
9	Cafeteria/Kitchen Consultant				
10	Fitness Center Consultant				
11	Art Consultant				
12	Security Consultant				
13	Mover/Moving Consultant				
		Subtotal	$0	$0	$0
		Fees Contingency	$0	$0	$0
		Total Fees	$0	$0	$0
E	**Tele/Data & Security**				
1	Telephone Equipmet				
2	Computer Equipment				
3	IT Network and Cable Mgmt				
4	Network Printers				
5	Cable				
6	Security Systems				
		Subtotal	$0	$0	$0
		Tel/Date Contingency	$0	$0	$0
		Total Tel, Data, Security	$0	$0	$0
F	**Furn, Equip, Moving**				
1	New Office Furniture				
2	New Workstations				
3	Miscellaneous Furniture				
4	Reworked Furniture				
5	AV Equipment				
6	Signage(Allowance)				
7	Artwork - Allowance				
8	Accessories & Plants				
9	Moving				
		Subtotal	$0	$0	$0
		Furn & Equipment, Moving Contingency	$0.00	$0.00	$0.00
		Total Furniture Equipment Moving	$0	$0	$0
		Project Contingency	$0	$0	$0
		TOTAL BUDGET ESTIMATE-Above Tenant Allowance	$0	$0	$0

Detailed Project Budget Form

	Expense Category	Description	Pre-Lease Budget	SD Budget QTY	Unit Cost	Est Total	Est $ $/RSF	DD Budget QTY	Unit Cost	Est Total	Est $ / RSF	Approved CM Bids	Cost / RSF	Final Final Costs	Cost / RSF
A	**Base Interior Fit-Up**														
1	Demolition														
2	Rough Carpentry														
3	Drywall														
4	Ceiling														
5	Millwork														
6	Glass/Mirror														
7	Hollow Metal														
8	Doors, Frames, and Hdw.														
9	HVAC														
10	Plumbing														
11	Sprinkler														
12	Lighting														
13	Electrical/Fire Alarm														
14	Flooring-yds.														
15	Wall Finishes														
16	Specialties														
17	IT Network and Cable Mgmt														
B	**Above Standard TI**														
1	Communicating Stair														
2	Fitness Center/Toilets/L Rms														
3	Cafeteria, etc.														
4	Floor Reinforcing														
5	Computer Room														
C	**Base Building Upgrades**														
1	Restrooms														
2	Main & Parkng Lobbies														
3	Elevators														
		Sub-Total Construction Costs	$0			$0	#REF!			$0	#REF!	$0	#REF!	$0	#REF!
		Construction Contingency	$0		$0.05										
		General Conditions	$0		$0.08										
		CM Fee	$0		$0.04										
		Insurance	$0		$0.01										
		Sales Tax on CM Services	$0		$0.06										
		Building Permit	$0		$0.01										
		Sub-Total CM Related Fees	$0.00												
		Projected Construction Costs	$0.00												
		Less Value of Landlord Contribution													
		Net (after allowance) Construction Costs	$0			$0	#REF!			$0	#REF!		#REF!	$0	#REF!
D	**Consultant Fees**														
1	Architect/Interior Design														
2	Owner's Rep/PM														
3	MEP Engineer														
4	Structural Engineer														
5	Lighting Consultant														
6	Acoustical Consultant														
7	AV Consultant														
8	IT Consultant														
9	Cafeteria/Kitchen Consultant														
10	Fitness Center Consultant														
11	Art Consultant														
12	Security Consultant														
13	Mover/Moving Consultant														
		Subtotal	$0			$0	#REF!			$0	#REF!		#REF!	$0.00	#REF!
		Fees Contingency													
		Total Fees	$0			$0	#REF!			$0	#REF!		#REF!	$0	#REF!
E	**Tele/Data & Security**														
1	Telephone Equipmet														
2	Computer Equipment														
3	IT Network and Cable Mgmt														
4	Network Printers														
5	Cable														
6	Security Systems														
		Subtotal	$0			$0	#REF!			$0	#REF!		#REF!	$0	#REF!
		Tel/Date Contingency													
		Total Tel, Data, Security	$0			$0	#REF!			$0	#REF!		#REF!	$0	#REF!
F	**Furn, Equip, Moving**														
1	New Office Furniture														
2	New Workstations														
3	Miscellaneous Furniture														
4	Reworked Furniture														
5	AV Equipment														
6	Signage (Allowance)														
7	Artwork - Allowance														
8	Accessories & Plants														
9	Moving														
		Subtotal	$0			$0	#REF!			$0	#REF!		#REF!	$0	#REF!
		Furn & Equipment, Moving Contingency													
		Total Furniture Equipment Moving	$0			$0	#REF!			$0	#REF!		#REF!	$0	#REF!
		TOTAL BUDGET ESTIMATE-Above Tenant Allowance	$0			$0	#REF!			$0	#REF!		#REF!	$0	#REF!

REVIEWING LEASE OR SALE DOCUMENTS

It used to be common for architects to read all leases and comment on the features. This service is now being done by the client's attorney with assistance from the project manager (PM) or owner's rep. Even though it is not often a part of the architect's scope and fee, I recommend the architect still review all dates that are in the lease/purchase agreement regarding:

- submission of client's plans
- description and timing of owner's work
- time for owner's review of client's plans
- lease start date
- contractor selection and approval process
- building rules and regulations

STORYBOARDING

After a property has been selected and the initial steps are complete, it is the perfect time to prepare a storyboard of the way you plan to move forward. The purpose of the storyboard is to outline the sequence of the steps and identify what is important in each step, including:

- When you want the other consultants to be available
- Timing of major decisions/presentations of plan concepts
- Furniture, IT, AV, and security involvement
- Preparation of updated budget and schedule
- Client reviews and approvals

There needs to be a good list of what is in SD and DD and a solid plan *not* to hand off DD plans until all/major planning and design decisions have been made.

The storyboard is an internal exercise intended to reduce or eliminate churn. (As you probably know, the word *churn* in the architectural world simply means redoing work that has been previously prepared and presented to the client.) The points in the process where churn naturally occurs are easy to identify. However, those points or situations are often hard to avoid because most everyone wants to go fast, skipping steps.

Churn occurs when planning is started without a well-defined program, without a well-defined budget, and especially without a detailed schedule.

Other than the Mechanical-Electrical-Plumbing (MEP) team, the other import-ant consultants, such as, IT, AV, security, lighting, and acoustical, must be on board at the beginning of the project so they can comment on the early conceptual plans. In addition, the client may have retained specialists or con-sultants for branding, art consulting, decorating, filing/storage, food service, or fitness. Churn happens when decisions are made, then rethought. Churn plays havoc on everyone's schedule and budget.

This first phase should end with a summary report describing the process that the team went through and events leading up to the decision of which property to lease, purchase for a new construction, or purchase for renovation or occupancy. The summary report should include client approvals of pre-liminary budgets and schedules and general guidelines of image and scope gathered in the envisioning.

REASSESS SCOPE AND CONTRACT AFTER THE INITIAL PHASE IS COMPLETE

This is not a typical phase, but it certainly should be. Often the selected build-ing, site, or space is considerably different from what was originally proposed. Perhaps market conditions were such that the client decided to purchase rath-er than lease, or to lease more space than initially needed which could be sublet for a period of time. This is a perfect opportunity to take a second look at the contract to see if any adjustments need to be made.

SCHEMATIC DESIGN

Programming Specifics: Philosophy, Culture, and Workflow

The second step in defining the client's needs happens after the building is selected and tested, and lease/purchase documents are finalized. The purpose of this phase is to understand the company's philosophy, desired quality of work, workflow, departmental adjacencies, workplace standards, and whether they follow grade levels of employees.

The architect documents all special areas like conference rooms, copy rooms, pantries, technology needs, and food service, in order to prepare draw-ings showing planning concepts, elevations, and sections.

These preliminary plans are most likely accompanied by freehand sketches or 3D wire frame drawings to get the client's approval on workflow, departmental adjacency, and special experience.

This program form, shown on page 57, was used to plan American Express's new headquarters in the World Financial Center in NYC. It is still our format for projecting a company's personnel and space needs. Programming was then and still is a two-step process: first, to work with the division presidents to project the growth of each of the businesses for the next five years, and second, to translate business growth to personnel needs. Based on approved standards, it was easy to project space needs. Special areas are then sized based on building population.

Staff projections are entered on the left side of the form and special areas for that group entered on the right side. After planning was complete, the division representatives kept the information up-to-date for future reference and replanning.

Here are some examples:

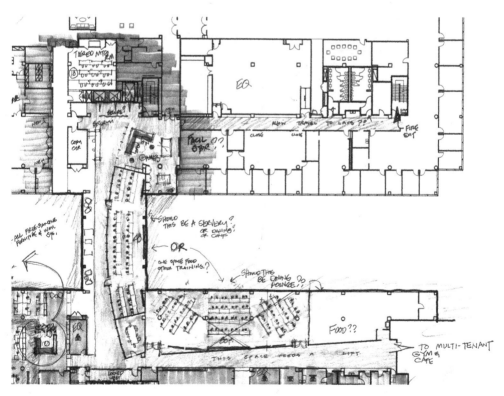

Sample freehand test fit.

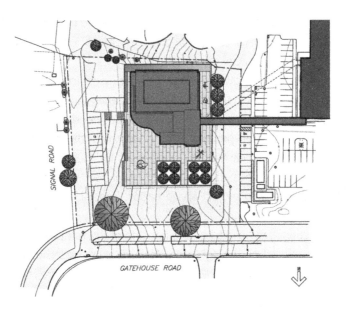

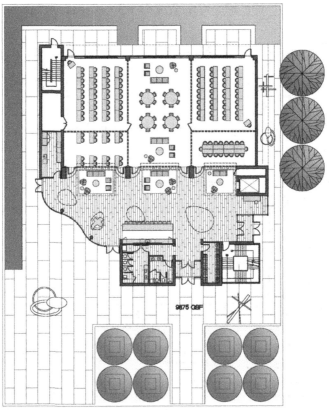

1st Floor

Sample SD presentation for a new building.

Sample SketchUp presentation for a new building.

DESIGN DEVELOPMENT: DEVELOPING THE APPROVED CONCEPTS

In this phase, the architect develops recommendations for building details, materials, colors, images, furniture recommendations, lighting concepts, and branding ideas.

Furniture

When projects begin, many clients have not decided how they will handle their furniture requirements. There are many scenarios. Outlined below is the most comprehensive scope.

If a client decides to purchase new furniture for a project, the process is quite detailed and the work process follows the architectural phases of SD, DD, and CD.

In the SD furniture phase:

- From the envisioning document, understand the client's workplace strategy, desired image, budget considerations, flexibility needs, and ways of working.
- From the conceptual plans, understand window and perimeter column spacing, column bay spacing, and depth of space from window to core.
- Recommend office and workplace standards for grade levels appropriate to the company.

- Recommend auxiliary furniture for support spaces such as conference/training rooms, informal work areas, benching, hoteling alternative office areas, cafeteria, or breakout areas.
- Select a level and quality of furniture and prepare a preliminary budget, based on the quantities required for the preliminary plan.
- Present the proposed standards and budget along with the architectural concept drawings.

In the DD furniture phase:

- Present specific manufacturer recommendations compatible with architectural design detailing, material selections, and image.
- Present finish and material selections for review.
- If the client has prearranged or national contracts with a manufacturer, obtain net/delivered/installed pricing for the required scope of work. It may be that the manufacturer has different price points or styles where budget options could be reviewed.
- If the client does not have a national contract, it is recommended to preselect three manufacturers who will evaluate your standards and plans and prepare budget estimates identifying list cost/discount/net cost/delivery and installation charge.
- Present the proposed standards and budgets along with the architectural Design Development drawings.
- Client selects standards and manufacturer and decides on costs.

In the CD furniture phase:

- Architect coordinates details and specifications with the selected manufacturer/local dealer and reviews final furniture drawings showing floor or wall power requirements that will be shown on the electrical plans.
- Architect reviews order for material selections and specifications and also detail parts list responsibility by local dealer.

In the construction furniture phase (when space is ready for installation):

- Architect reviews installation, prepares punch list for dealer review of any missing or damaged product, and signs off for payment.
- Architect delivers warranty information to client.

There are obviously a number of other options where the architect's furniture services will need to be modified for each situation. The furniture process is quite detailed and takes time to coordinate thoroughly with the architectural work. Furniture manufacturers use smart symbols to prepare the final plans and are able to do accurate take-offs for budgeting and installation. Architects should incorporate these correct symbols on their final drawings to test clearances and quantities.

Mechanical, Electrical, Plumbing, Fire Protection (MEP)

It is critical for the MEP team to be selected and on board prior to site or building selection. MEP costs often represent more than half the construction costs and as such are critical to understand and compare for each building being evaluated.

The most appropriate approach is to send out an RFP to a few firms for this initial phase of work. The selected firm will be involved in the Pre-Lease/Pre-Purchase phase along with the architect as buildings or sites are evaluated. Only when a building/site has been selected will the MEP scope of work be able to be determined. At that time, the architect could negotiate fees with the firm on board to complete the SD, DD, CD, and CA phases, or go out with a new RFP to a few firms for competitive bidding.

MEP in the SD phase:

- Understand base building MEP systems
- Recommend mechanical upgrades, if required, to meet client needs
- Prepare single line mechanical drawings showing equipment locations and duct runs
- Evaluate electrical service to building and capacity—main electrical entrance room plus service to floors

- Determine if a generator is required; if so, propose location of generator plus fuel tank location
- Evaluate condition of plumbing piping and toilet rooms
- Evaluate fire protection system, floor control, and distribution
- Coordinate preparation of MEP budget with architect

MEP in the DD phase:

- Review approved schematic architectural plans
- Finalize single line concept drawings with architectural plans
- Prepare outline specs for each trade for pricing upgrade
- Update MEP budget with architect

MEP in the CD phase:

- Review architectural background drawings
- Prepare CDs for each of the disciplines
- Coordinate CDs with architect and other consultants
- Prepare final specs
- Make final code check of systems

MEP in the CA phase:

- Attend weekly project meetings
- Review schedule and completion of work
- Prepare systems punch list
- Prepare and submit as-built drawings
- Prepare close-out schedules and commissioning

FINAL CODE REVIEW

The time to do the final code review is after Design Development is approved and prior to Construction Documents starting. You can link to a detailed list of items tracked in each category.

The major categories of work reviewed for each project:

- Walking surfaces
- Doors and doorways
- Ramps
- Curb ramps
- Elevators
- Parking
- Passenger loading zones
- Stairways
- Handrails
- Drinking fountains
- Toilet and bathing rooms
- Water closets
- Toilet compartments
- Ambulatory accessible compartments
- Urinals, toilets, and sinks

DESIGN HANDOFF FOR PRODUCTION OF CDs

The issues most project managers have with processes and schedules, especially where there are major handoffs, are always the same. For example, the DD to CD handoff is extremely difficult because it often involves a number of firms. The first handoff is from the internal staff to the production staff. When backgrounds are complete, there is a handoff from the architectural firm to the structural engineer and the MEP group. Other handoffs follow to the consulting firms as they build more detail onto the plans. The accuracy of the base plan is critical from a number of points of view. If a new base plan has to be issued, the Structural Engineer or MEP firms may have to redo previously completed work and *may* ask for an extra. It is never possible for the architect to go back to the client to ask for a change order, especially if the change was the architect's fault. Perhaps even more challenging than the loss of efficiency and costs is the loss of time in making the changes.

Handoffs are serious business, no matter in what phase they occur. It is important for the firm to understand and document the different requirements between internal handoffs and external handoffs. With internal handoffs, the team members delivering information need to be clear about what they will be delivering. The group receiving the information is responsible to let the other group know what they are expecting to receive so there is no misunderstanding as to scope and timing.

CD STORYBOARD

It is important to take a few minutes to produce another storyboard outlining the difficult "must do" items required on each drawing. Having said that, there are rules that should apply to all projects:

1. There should be a team review from DD to CD prior to starting the CD phase. The firm should insist that material, finish, and detail decisions be made prior to starting CDs. Build time in the schedule for a successful handoff.
2. The CD process should start with a storyboard identifying all the special CD needs, such as:
   - What's needed by engineers (so you don't have to send them updated backgrounds)
   - Dimensioning technique
   - List of required details
   - Long lead items clearly identified
   - Details described using SketchUp/Revit capabilities
   - Freehand mark up of DD plans showing material breaks
   - Approved furniture plans
   - Standard Telephone/Electirc (T/E) plans including standard dimensioning of outlet for offices and workstations
   - Ceiling breaks and visuals of details
   - Glass front selections with details
   - Work done by others shown on plan and identified as NIC—not in contract
   - List of what doesn't need to be drawn

Checking CDs before they go out is the best way to avoid extras during construction.

CONSTRUCTION DOCUMENTS

When a project gets to the documentation phase, the tone of the project changes, since the client is not as involved. The CD team is now on its own, often on the hot seat to produce a good set of CDs while trying to stay on schedule. Let us presume all architectural product and material specs were checked for availability prior to being presented to the client in the DD presentations. If the time frame from initial DD presentations to completion of CDs has been a few months, it may make sense to do a double check on availability for those must-have products. I recommend using a Long Lead Item Checklist, similar to the chart on the following page, to track the specified products for each discipline. Even if it is not necessary to do a double check, it is recommended the form be filled in *prior to* signing up a GC or CM.

What you do not want to happen is the contractor coming back to the client weeks into the project saying the lights, wallcovering, or carpet that was specified is not available and a substitution needs to be made.

The contractor should have checked product availability during the bidding phase and made out POs for all long lead items, to implement if they are awarded the contract.

CONSTRUCTION PHASE: BIDDING

Most clients want or require bids to be taken for each construction project. The selection of a contractor on repeat business is most often predetermined, unless they did not do a good job on a prior project. For a small percentage of our projects, where a contractor list is prepared, the architect, client, and PM/owner's rep each may make recommendations as to who should be on the list. It is important to try to have a level playing field in all bidding.

There are good reasons why we all have favorites and try to get our friends on the list:

- The firm helped us develop the preconstruction costs
- The firm helped us develop construction costs on other projects and was not selected
- This project may have potential extras, and this contractor dealt fairly with extras
- The contractor "watches our back" and makes us look good, working out missteps or omissions
- The firm built another similar project for us that was very successful
- The client was pleased with prior work the firm has done for them
- They recommend us for work

Long Lead Item Checklist

	Construction Item	Manufacturer Model	Item Description	Subcontractor or Vendor	Contact Phone No.	Anticipated Lead Time From Order	Date Ordered	Delivery Date	Status
A.	**Metals**								
1	Hollow Metal Doors	ABC Metals	Welded HM Frames	XYZ Installer	(914) 555-5555	8 weeks	5-Jan-01	6-Mar-01	On Time
2	Hollow Metal Frames								
3	Structural Steel								
4	Misc. Metals								
B.	**Carpentry**								
5	Architectural Millwork								
6	Architectural Casework								
7	Solid Core Wood Doors								
8	Special Doors								
9	Finish Hardware								
C.	**Interior Finishes**								
10	Drywall Specialties								
11	Acoustical Ceiling								
12	Ceiling Specialties								
13	Glass and Glazing								
14	Acoustical Treatments								
15	Ceramic Tile								
16	Resilient Flooring (VCT)								
17	Resilient Base								
18	Stone Flooring								
19	Wood Flooring								
20	Carpet								
21	Wallcovering								
22	Specialty Wall Finish								
23	Window Treatments								
D.	**Architectural Specialties**								
24	Toilet Accessories								
25	Kitchen Appliances								
26	Marker Boards								
27	Projection Screens								
28	Audio Visual Equipment								
29	Movable Partition								
30	Signs								
31	Fire Extinguishers								
32	Raised Flooring								
E.	**Mechanical**								
33	Air Handlers								
34	Condenser Units								
35	Packaged Units								
36	Instruments / Controls								
37	Thermostats								
38	Exhaust Fans								
39	Exhaust Hood								
40	Specialty Ductwork								
41	Linear Diffusers								
F.	**Plumbing**								
42	Fixtures								
43	Water Heater								
44	Sprinkler Equipment								
45	Instruments / Controls								
46	Pre-Action Controls								
G.	**Electric**								
47	Light Fixtures								
48	Light Switches								
49	Dimming Switches								
50	Dimming Systems								
51	Exit Lights								
52	Emergency Lights								
53	Fire Alarm Devices								
54	Fire Alarm Control Panel								
H.	**Other**								
55	Access Control System								
56	Access Control Devices								
57	Security CCTV								

Bidding can be tricky if the process is not clear. If the Instructions to Bidders are not clear, allowing each contractor to bid his or her own way, it is very difficult to level the bids.

Here are some tough questions that should be asked of the bidders:

- What do you include in your general conditions?
- How do you apportion your company's insurance policy premium across projects?
- What normal general conditions costs do you ask subs to include in their bid? For instance, trade cleaning, protection, and final cleaning prior to move in?
- Are you willing to having an "open book"—where the client views what subs charge and what you pay? How do you handle trade buyouts and final costs?
- If you buy out a trade for less than included in your bid, do you reimburse the client?
- What omissions do you see in our drawings that could lead to extras? Where do we need to provide more detail?
- How do you handle review and early ordering of long lead items so there will not be substitutions?

Bid Format

Bid response formats should be included in all bid packages so bidders respond to the RFP in a similar way for easy comparison and leveling of the numbers. A sample GC/CM questionnaire follows.

THE PUNCH LIST

Most construction contracts have a clause that requires the contractor to show "substantial completion" before they can receive final payment for the work. Substantial completion is defined by the AIA as "when the Work, or designated portion thereof, is sufficiently complete in accordance with the Contract Documents so the Owner can occupy or utilize the Work for its intended use." Substantial completion is an important, but often overlooked, term in construction contracts. It is significant because it is also often used as a trigger in construction contracts for a number of important events. Some of these events include:

GC / CM Questionairre

	Category	Preferred Answer	Candidate A		Candidate B	
1	**About the Firm**		PTS		PTS	
a	Type of Firm	Full Service CM				
b	Age of Firm	10 - 15 Years				
c	Location of Office	< 15 minutes to site				
d	Number of Employees	> 20 professional staff				
e	Typical Type of Work	Base Bldg./Interiors				
f	Typical Sized Project	> 50,000 s.f.				
g	To what extent will the principal be involved in the project? None, Minimal, Regular, Heavy	Regularly				
i	Average Number of Staff Proposed for the Team	4				
j	Workload during the Extent of the Project	Average				
k	(Minimal, Average, Heavy)					
l	Ability to Properly Handle Project with Present Workload - Easy, Moderate, Difficult	Easy				
n	Experience with Partnering with Other Design Firms -	Regularly				
2	**Specific Project Information**		PTS		PTS	
a	Prior Experience with Proposed Landlord/Developer	Yes				
b	Familiar with Project Workletters and Landlord Const. Stds	Yes				
c	Prior Experience with Architect	Yes				
d	Prior Experience with Remote Client Contact	Yes				
e	Ability to Start Preconstruction Services Immediately	Yes				
f	Perceived Ability to Work with Project Key Contacts	Satisfactory				
g	Workload of Project Key Contacts	Light				
h	Innovation Displayed in Interview (if applicable)	Interesting				
i	Experience in High Rise Office Buildings in	Yes				
j	Flexibility to Work with Schedule and Scope Changes	Flexible				
k	Experience with Data Center Construction	Yes				
l	Ability to Obtain Performance Bond in Amount Required	Yes				
m	Any past, pending or ongoing legal disputes?	No				
3	**Fees - Tenant Fit-up Work**		PTS		PTS	
a	General Conditions (Reimbursables) - Not to Exceed % of Work	6.00%				
b	CM Services Fee - Fixed % of Work including Gen. Conditions	3.00%				
c	Total % Mark-up over Sub Costs (3a+3b above)	**9.18%**				
d	Cost to Procure Performance Bond					
4	**Fees - Changes to Scope**		PTS		PTS	
a	General Conditions (Reimbursables) - Not to Exceed % of Work	6.00%				
b	CM Services Fee - Fixed % of Work including Gen. Conditions	2.00%				
c	Total % Mark-up over Sub Costs (3a+3b above)	**8.12%**				
5	**Fees - Average Mark-up for all Categories**		PTS		PTS	
a	Fees Based on a Project Completion Date of	**8.65%**				
b	Average Hourly Rates of Team Members (US Dollars)	$80.00				
c	Proposed Compensation if Project is Terminated? (T&M, Lump sum)	Time & Materials				
6	**RFP Response**		PTS		PTS	
a	Was a description of the firm included?	Yes				
b	Were relevant references included?	Yes				
d	How did references check out?	Exceptional				
e	Is full scope of services included in base fee?	Yes				
f	Are any of the basic services excluded or additional? (Provide list)	No				
g	Is insurance certificate provided with requested limitations?	Yes				
h	Was the fee proposal broken down properly?	Yes				
i	Were additional services addressed?	Yes				
j	Were hourly rates received?	Yes				
k	Was the proposal received on time?	Yes				
l	Was the proposal received in the format requested?	Yes				
m	Was team's approach to this project discussed?	Yes				
n	Were résumés of the proposed team members provided?	Yes				
o	Was proposal organized and well thought out?	Yes				
p	Were examples of similar projects provided?	Yes				
	Total Score		0		0	

- when certain limitation periods begin to run on a contractor's claims under the construction contract
- when certain warranty periods commence
- when the owner takes over responsibility for utilities, insurance, etc., for the project
- perhaps most important from the contractor's perspective, when the contractor is entitled to payment of the contract balance, less retainage funds to be withheld until final completion

To request substantial completion, the contractor submits a list of items, called a "punch list," to the architect indicating what he/she thinks remains to be finished. At issue is usually the definition of "ready for Owner's intended use." It is then for the architect, engineers, and other consultants to determine, with the approval of their client, if in fact the remaining items are minor in nature.

Another test of "ready for Owner's intended use" is whether a Certificate of Occupancy has been issued, indicating that the facility is up to code and all systems are in place and operational.

The best way to avoid conflict at the end of the project is to work out in advance a definition suitable to the client, architect, and contractor. At issue is usually how much annoyance the client is willing to put up with contractors in their space finishing their work.

The earlier the contractor starts the final punch list, the more items there will be on the list. Architects would like to wait until there are only a few items remaining so they do not have to come back time after time. It can be very time-consuming for the architects and others to prepare the list, return to check off the completed items, revise the list if required, and keep returning until all items are checked off.

The difference between the facility being ready for the owner to occupy and use the space and *all* the work delivered, installed, and completed in accordance with the plans is very subjective. The contractor can start the list; however, it should be checked and then gone over by the consultant team to be finalized. The list should be prepared in such a way as to be able to be sorted by building, floor, room, and trade for easy review by the contractor and subs. It is not recommended for the architect and others to use the original contractor's list without proper review of all trades' work.

 I am frequently asked if the client should be involved in the punch list process. I would answer both yes and no. Yes, the client should be aware of the list, but no, they should not necessarily walk room to room with the consultants. However, I think it is human nature that when the contractor and subcontractors know the client is aware of the items on the list of what needs to be finished, they will perform at a higher level, especially if there is a possibility for future work. Subcontractors have a lot to lose if they do not perform well at the end of the project. If they do not finish their work perfectly, they may not get future work from the contractor, architect, or client.

One of the difficulties with preparing the final punch list is that many of the subcontractors are already off the job by the time the punch list starts and will need to be called back if there are any items for them to fix or finish. This is very painful for the subcontractor. For this reason, the architect and the contractor should make note of the trades that finish their work early and prepare punch lists for those trades as they happen, rather than waiting for the final punch list. This would eliminate many issues at the end of the job.

For those trades finishing their work early, I always recommend they get the contractor's approval that their work was completed, in accordance with the plans and specs, before they leave the jobsite. They should also take photos of their completed work.

Three primary trades are at the mercy of others for keeping their completed work in good order:

- Ceilings—The ceiling grid and often the tiles are installed early in the construction process. Many trades follow that need to work in the ceiling plenum and will remove tiles or cut holes in the sheetrock to install mechanical, electrical, AV, or security devices. The ceiling contractor should take photos of their work and be reimbursed to come back to repair the ceiling.
- Flooring—Wood, stone, ceramic, or vinyl tile is often installed while trades are working overhead. It is easy for these finished materials to be soiled or scratched even when protected by heavy paper. Once again, photos should be taken of completed work to protect the subcontractor from having to come back to make repairs for free. Trades are generally very respectful of others' work, but accidents do happen.
- Painting—Primed or finished painted walls get marred or scratched all the time. Unless there are cameras all around the space, it is impossible to find out who scratched the finished

walls. Regardless, it should not be the painter who has to pay to fix them, unless the painter was given a special allowance for touch-up painting.

Just prior to move-in there are other groups, working for the client, not the contractor, that come in to install sound systems, AV, IT, telephone, or internet devices in ceilings. These groups need to be made aware of the existing conditions and be responsible for their work.

When the client has access to the status of the punch list, it is a perfect marketing opportunity for the architect and even the contractor to show how diligent they are in working to get everything done prior to move-in.

So what is on a typical punch list? It is usually all the products and finishes that make the project "sing." Here is a sampling of the types of items found on most lists:

- Long lead items that did not get ordered in time to get installed
- Long lead items that got substituted and did not get delivered on time
- Product specification changes by client
- Product additions by client
- Products that got damaged in shipment
- Work damaged by others
- Sloppy workmanship
- Touch-up painting
- Carpet and tile cleaning
- Hardware adjustments
- Replacing damaged or soiled ceiling tiles

MOVE-IN

Move-in time is another opportunity for the architect to show the client how well the project went. Everyone wants repeat business. Moves are usually over a weekend, often a long holiday weekend, and all systems need to be up and running by the next Monday.

 For the architect, being available over the weekend is not usually a part of the contract scope, but it is very comforting for the employees and management to see the architects there to answer any questions.

There is a lot for the architect to do, including finishing the construction punch list, reviewing the furniture punch list, testing some of the AV/sound systems, making sure the appliances are plugged in and operational, and most important, placing "Move Trouble Tags" on each desk so employees can turn them in if they find anything that needs attention.

CLOSE-OUT

Most consultants have a clause in their contracts about supplying as-built architectural and MEP drawings at the end of the job. Having a set of accurate plans is certainly important to the client, but do not forget about all the other things that are necessary for the contractor to review with the client so they know how to manage the facility over the life of the lease or building occupancy.

If your client owns and occupies the building, there are a number of building management systems for which the client needs to have training in "operational management." There are also interior systems that the staff needs to have knowledge of for efficient day-to-day use of the facility. Each category of systems needs to be documented in a working manual in terms of use, scheduled maintenance, repair, and warranty.

Building Systems	Interior Systems
Building Management System (BMS)	Acoustical sound masking
	Audiovisual
Doors/Keys/Locks	Cleaning guidelines
Electrical	Client acceptance reports
Fire prevention	Conference calling
Generator/Uninterrupted Power Supply (UPS)	Construction logs
	Furniture
HVAC system	Kitchen pantry appliances
Landscaping/Sprinkler	Lighting (lamps and dimming)
Pest control	Operations manuals
Plumbing	Product attic stock
Product warranties	Supplemental HVAC units
Security	Technology
Sprinkler	Video conferencing

For larger clients, it is best when the architect or furniture dealer loads their plans into a Facility Management system, so the client can:

- Track and report on where everyone is sitting
- Keep furniture plans up to date
- Track and report on vacant workplace and office locations
- Track and report on departmental areas for chargeback
- Track and report on moves, adds, and changes
- Prepare test fits for future renovations

CHAPTER 7

Day 2 Services

STAYING IN TOUCH WITH THE CLIENT

I highly recommend that architects explore adding Day 2 services to their basic architectural services. Most Day 2 services can be subscription-based services; these are normally paid monthly or yearly on a contracted lump sum basis.

All of the services listed below have to do with commercial architecture, not residential work.

DATA MANAGEMENT FOR OWNED OR LEASED FACILITIES (A SERVICE TO THE ARCHITECT'S CLIENT)

Architects designing single-use office buildings, multitenanted office buildings, or architectural interiors can help their clients track and report on their owned or leased data. Real estate firms have been providing this service to tenants and building owners for many years. There is no reason architects should not also provide this service. Architects can use many products to provide this service. The easiest-to-use and most popular product is Link Systems' application called ProLease.

This system includes over 120 standard reports, such as:

- FASB lease accounting
- Rent payments
- Budgeting and forecasting
- Critical dates and email alarms
- Retail features
- Document management
- Location mapping
- Charting and graphing

ProLease staff will set up the client's database, enter the data, and give the architect and owner complete access to the data and reports.

This service helps the architect stay in the loop for Day 2 work. Architects can use a single ProLease version to enter as many clients' data as they want—with each client having total access and security on their account information.

Over 700 of the country's largest Fortune 1000 corporations and the top real estate firms use ProLease.

PORTFOLIO MANAGEMENT (A SERVICE FOR THE BUILDING OWNER)

Every building owner needs accurate base building plans, building measurements, and marketing plans. Architects can assist owners with test fits for prospective tenants; upkeep of tenant-demising plans, color-coded by lease expiration; building area analysis; and tenant RSF calculations.

A few companies have systems to do this. Link Systems provides these services for the architect and their clients. The architect can invoice the clients directly on a monthly basis for the following services:

- CAD floor plans
- Field surveys
- Marketing plans
- Acquisition analysis
- Stacking plans
- EAP fire safety plans
- RSF measurements
- PlanBook updates
- Loss factor analysis

WORKPLACE/FACILITY MANAGEMENT (A SERVICE FOR THE ARCHITECT'S INTERIOR DESIGN CLIENT)

When an architect assists a company with an interior renovation or relocation, this Day 2 service helps them efficiently track and report on moves, adds, and changes, including:

- Updated seating charts
- Personnel moves
- Department allocations
- Space utilization
- Workplace reporting

These services enable the architect to maintain an active, strategic partner relationship with the client for that project and may lead to future projects in other locations. Link Systems can set up the architect's plans in the Workplace module.

CAP X SERVICES (SERVICES FOR THE ARCHITECT'S CORPORATE CLIENTS)

A part of all large companies' annual budget planning process includes estimates of capital expenditures for the next year. A major part of the planned expenditures often relates to real estate and facilities' planned renovations, additions, or scheduled maintenance.

A comprehensive list by building, prepared by the company's facility manager, architect, MEP engineer, and contractor, should represent the team's backlog for the next year. These projects are often awarded without competitive bidding.

PART IV

Moving On Up—From Intern to Architect

CHAPTER 8

RFPs and Proposals

The transition from Intern to Architect is a very positive and dramatic time. When you pass your exam and can put "AIA" after your name, you should certainly celebrate. In Part II, planning for the AIA exam, I describe all the positive things that should happen to you, including:

1. The firm should give you a new title and will bill you out at a higher rate. (If that is the case, do not forget to ask for a raise.)
2. Having more licensed/registered architects on the company roster looks better for the firm when a potential client is looking at the company's website
3. RFPs (Requests for Proposal) often ask the question, "How many licensed/registered architects are in the firm and will be assigned to the project?"

As one moves up through the organization, one of the most important functions is learning how to evaluate and prepare responses to RFIs and RFPs. In smaller and midsize firms, principals should welcome help with the preparation of RFPs and RFIs, since that is a very time-consuming activity. Larger firms have individuals dedicated to marketing and proposal writing. A side benefit of helping with proposal writing is you get to know much more about the firm, including the in-depth ideas of the principals, metrics of past projects, marketing strategies, and how to calculate proposed fees.

RFPs AND PROPOSALS

The architecture business is always changing, and because of that, it is so important to be ready for anything. A significant change happened in the mid 1990s when the owner's rep and project manager business started. In many cases, these newly formed firms became the internal real estate and facilities groups for large corporations. In the good ol' days, RFPs (Requests for Proposal) were sent out by the real estate or facilities groups, and architectural firms would have a couple of weeks to prepare responses. After reviewing responses, the client would then invite a short list of firms to make presentations. Based on the firms' proposals and presentations, there would be negotiations with one or more firms to make sure they understood scope, quality, and timing; then a decision was made.

Another big change happened during the same period. Larger corporations started including the purchasing department—newly renamed as the procurement department—in the RFP process. This group not only reviewed the proposals, but also negotiated the work. Most of us thought the change was in name only, but were to find out there was in fact a difference in responsibilities.

Matt Lim defines the two names in this way: "Procurement involves the process of selecting vendors, establishing payment terms, strategic vetting and selection, the negotiation of contracts, and actual purchasing of goods. Procurement is concerned with acquiring (procuring) all of the goods, services, and work that are vital to an organization. Procurement is, essentially, the overarching or umbrella term within which purchasing can be found."[2]

This change affected not only the quality of the RFP, but also the quality of the process. The focus changed from the real estate or facilities group trying to select the "best firm" to do the work, to the procurement group looking for the "least cost alternative." When the firms bidding are perceived to be equals, why wouldn't it make sense to select the lowest cost? As a bidder, you know when the decision comes down to price, only two things can happen:

1. You lose the business to someone cheaper
2. You win the business because you are cheaper, but have loads of work and are underpaid

This is what happens when you are perceived to be a vendor. *This is a terrible way to buy professional services.* When your fees take precedence over quality of services and experience, you are in a race to the bottom.

To make matters even worse, firms are sometimes requested to make presentations even *before* the RFP is sent out. Architects who respond know little or nothing about the client or project, hoping that they will somehow make the

2 Matt Lim, "What Is the Difference between Procurement and Purchasing?," *Procurify*, accessed April 19, 2018, https://blog.procurify.com/2014/02/07/what-is-the-difference-between-procurement-and-purchasing/

short list and get an RFP. In Chapter 12, I discuss the importance of being the strategic service partner.

Making a presentation *before* you know anything about the type/size/location of the project is risky. You might show your cool stuff, only to find out they want a budget job, or vice versa. Murphy's Law says we will probably guess wrong. In either case, architects get little to no time to prepare their responses, so they must have good information readily available.

It is critical that you have accurate information about past projects. Plans, construction costs, furniture costs, SF metrics, products, team members, and so forth are critical to include in RFPs or during presentations.

I remember making a presentation to a large company that was relocating their headquarters. I did my due diligence before the presentation. I checked out their website, company history, and management team, and even looked at their online company store where employees could buy shirts, hats, and branded goods. Everything pointed to a company interested in having a facility that maximized the needs of the employee. My pitch included a lot about workplace efficiency, employee retention, and amenities. I was so off-base.

As I finished, I asked if there were any questions, and the CFO said, "Nice pitch, but we are looking for the firm that can do the cheapest construction drawings."

RFIs AND RFPs

There are two main types of project requests:

1. An RFI—Request for Information
2. An RFP—Request for Proposal

The difference between the two is significant but often misunderstood by the client, the procurement group, or consultant soliciting a proposal from the architect.

Think of an RFI as being similar to a preproposal. RFIs are very frustrating to receive and respond to, especially after reading all the information they are asking you to provide. RFIs are requesting information about your firm's history, staffing, and project types, sizes, and costs. The RFIs only include the bare minimum to let you know you are being considered for an architectural project.

RFIs even have questions about the firm's financials, salaries, and tax records. At the end of the document, some even ask for a fee proposal.

RFIs are usually boilerplate documents asking the firm to answer very basic questions about the firm. After you receive a few of these, you begin to know all the questions and should have the answers ready to pop into their response format. For my company, I created a "response generator" PowerPoint presentation that had every question we'd been asked and our typical response. RFIs are easy to respond to if you have all your facts together, such as size of firm, types of staff, number of projects by type and size, who is assigned to each, and costs per USF/RSF. RFIs also ask for information regarding the timing of projects, AV, IT, security, acoustics, lighting, and furniture.

An RFP attempts to describe the client and their proposed project goals and objectives. The best RFPs are those where the client and their realtor, project manager, or owner's rep take the time to think about the project and *describe what they are planning to do*. An RFP may not include all the details, but it describes as specifically as possible what the client is looking for in terms of image, growth, location, and culture. It is nice to know how the client's business has grown from a staff or product/service point of view. The more we know about the way a potential client works, such as visitor needs, design intent, ratio of offices to open stations, or furniture needs, the better our idea of the type of client they will be, and the amount of time we will have to spend.

In either case, it is difficult to calculate a fixed fee with a limited amount of information. That is why we always recommend that the client break the project into two phases: first, developing a scope document, and second, the implantation plan. The scope document should always be a fixed fee assignment.

We try to find out as much as we can about the potential client by looking at their website, Facebook, LinkedIn, and Instagram pages, as well as their blogs.

Look for *connections* to use in your presentation. For example:

- Who is on their management team?
- Where did they go to school?
- How long have they been with the company?
- What were their last jobs?
- How many offices does the company have?
- What architect did they use on their last project?
- Were they happy with that architect?

- Who was their realtor/contractor/owner's rep/furniture dealer on prior projects? Give them a call to find out all you can.
- If you know anyone who has done prior work for the client, ask what he or she thinks of your chances.
- Is this company in the same industry group as any of your other clients?
- What are the metrics for their type of business? You may be asked about RSF per person and costs per RSF.

Why is this important? Most recipients first read the opening or summary pages of your RFP and then flip to the fee section. In the first paragraph, you should include a letter of appreciation for being considered, and something about why you are the perfect firm to help them with this project. The details do not matter to them at this point. Second, you will need to know all the basics about the project when you are asked to make a presentation.

Unfortunately, calculating the fee is virtually impossible at this point, even when there is a detailed RFP. It was always my best guess in terms of scope, timing, or budget. At this point, estimating costs and profit to determine the fee is difficult.

Imagine going into a car dealership and asking how much a car costs. You would never do it without first giving the dealer some specifics about what you are looking for. Why then are architects always expected to give a fee without specifics? Answer: *Firms are willing to provide a fee without specifics.*

If we used the time spent on similar projects to estimate future work, we would probably never get the job! Fees are usually calculated based on who else is bidding, current market conditions, how badly we need the work, whether the proposal is tight or not well written with the probability of extra costs, among other things.

Understanding your firm's metrics is critical so you know when to zig or zag.

Often the RFP contains a format for entering the fee information. Even if the formats are cumbersome and the questions asked seem meaningless, always follow the format.

Firms are often asked about the staff they will assign to each phase, how many hours they will spend, and what the fee will be for each phase of work. Make your answer look reasonable—there is no right answer.

Sometimes clients ask for fees to be quoted in terms of cost per usable square foot instead of cost per rentable square foot. By doing this, firms cannot take advantage of the normally large building loss factor. For the same reason, but in reverse, building owners quote rental rates in term of rentable square feet instead of usable square feet; their rental number looks smaller.

If we adjust the fee up to reflect the loss factor, then the fee will look very high, and we may be enticed to lower it. That is their hope. Before you enter the fee, try to understand what they are really looking for.

Questions about fees in the RFP are difficult to answer because, at this point, there is not much known about the project. The firm that guesses the lowest fee usually has the upper hand.

Another point is that even a well-prepared RFP may not say much about security, technology, AV, new vs. reused furniture, custom design elements, or millwork. If you take those categories of work into account, your fee may be much higher than others'. Be careful to only price what you have been asked to price, and not what you know or think will be needed.

I used to estimate our time for a "complete job," even when I knew they forgot to ask about all aspects of the scope. I do not do that anymore. If the RFP is not clear, I exclude that work and call it an "additional service" so it is clear starting out if scope is not included in the fee. Caution: Be aware that this approach may appear negative because it may give the impression that you are going to nickel-and-dime them on every little thing. Sometimes the work excluded looks greater than the work being included.

Keep in mind if the client has retained a project manager (PM) or an owner's rep, they sell their services from a different point of view.

If the client does not have an in-house team of specialists, the PM or owner's rep indicates he can perform as the client's in-house team to interview or recommend other consultants, manage the project from a schedule and budget point of view, review invoices, etc. If the RFP does not describe the services of the PM or owner's rep, *ask the questions,* so services are not duplicated. Architects should make it very clear in their contract about which services will be done by the PM or owner's rep and those he will *not* be required to do.

Some owner's reps and PMs like the consultants to work through them, limiting the contact the consultant has with the client. *This is never a good idea.* Whenever possible, you want to be able to have direct contact with your client so you can build a relationship.

Having said that, owner's reps and PMs can be a tremendous help in running the project and, fortunately, most are.

RESPONDING TO AN RFP OR RFI

Most proposals state that you need to follow the RFP format, and you should. If you do not, it is an easy way to get yourself and your firm disqualified. However, before you start answering an RFP, it is a good idea to do two things:

Evaluate Your Chances of Being Selected

Human nature is to want to "win" all projects—no matter what. Even if it were possible to win all projects, the reality is that some will be too big, some too small, and others not the right type. We developed the following format for evaluating our chances after a series of serious mishaps when our strategy backfired. We won a number of projects where we did not have either sufficient experience or staff, or the timing did not mesh well with our other projects. Fortunately, there were no disasters, but many narrow escapes, and we learned a number of valuable lessons.

Our evaluation format is divided into two sections and our grading system is similar to the way many products are rated:

- Type of Project
- Type of Client

If Your Decision to Respond Is *Yes*

Prepare a quick outline of the material you want to include in your response. Give yourself enough time to do a good job researching the company and writing your response. If you wait until the day before the RFP is due to start the process, your response will not be well done or on time.

Use a chart like the one on page 99. Mark your answers, then count your smiley faces and divide by 26:

- Fewer than 2.0 smiley faces, run for the hills
- Between 2.0 and 3.0 smiley faces, you need a great proposal
- Over 3.0 smiley faces, you have a great chance of winning

A few things are important to look for when you review an RFP. RFPs often come with no advanced notice like a phone call or an email. You are only given a day or two to accomplish a number of tasks:

1. Acknowledge that you received it and are going to respond.

2. Sign a nondisclosure agreement.

3. Agree to a walk-through of either the client's existing or pro-posed space. Walk-throughs are interesting because you often get to meet the other firms being evaluated. Walk-throughs are also tricky because the client wants the people to attend who are going to work on the project. Since you may only get two days' notice, the individuals you want on the project might not be available.

4. Understand when they want the RFP in their hands. For instance, they might say the proposal is due by Friday the 5th at 9:00 AM, but in another section they say that they want hard copies as well as digital copies on the 5th at 9:00 AM. That means the proposal really needs to go in the mail on the 3rd, since it takes one day with FedEx or UPS to get there, plus a day to get from their mailroom to the person(s) reading it. Be careful when using FedEx or UPS services. Even if you ask for next day AM delivery, the project meeting may occur before FedEx delivers. Check to see if the address given meets FedEx or UPS standards with a real address, not a PO Box, and has the right zip code and tele-phone number associated with it.

5. If the company requesting the proposal asks for numerous cop-ies, you need to plan for extra printing time.

6. When you are asked to email digital versions, there are two things to consider. First, make sure you have a correct email address, and second, can the user's email system take the large files you may be sending? (If not, see if you can send it through a service that allows you to send large files such as Dropbox .com or WeTransfer.com.) Always send a proposal in .pdf format.

7. Discuss internally the way you want the printed version bound so you can make sure to have all the binding materials on hand.

8. Don't forget to make extra copies of the proposal for your team to take to the presentation, plus one or two extra copies for folks who might come to the meeting unannounced.

9. Last, we always have questions because the information we need is hardly ever complete in the RFP. It is important to get these questions answered early so you get responses back in time if you need to modify your scope and fee.

Questions About Project	No 1	2	3	4	Yes 5
Have we successfully completed projects of this type?	☺	☺	☺	☺	☺
Have we successfully completed projects of this size?	☺	☺	☺	☺	☺
Have we successfully completed projects in our locale?	☺	☺	☺	☺	☺
Do we have experienced staff available to do the work?	☺	☺	☺	☺	☺
Will our support staff have a big learning curve?	☺	☺	☺	☺	☺
Does the timing match with our staff availability?	☺	☺	☺	☺	☺
Will our staff be excited if we get the assignment?	☺	☺	☺	☺	☺
Were our past projects of this type profitable?	☺	☺	☺	☺	☺
Is this a type project that could be published?	☺	☺	☺	☺	☺
Were our past projects of this type photographed?	☺	☺	☺	☺	☺
Are there projects of this type in our marketplace?	☺	☺	☺	☺	☺
Do we know consultants who would be good to use?	☺	☺	☺	☺	☺
Does this project come with an Owner's Rep or PM?	☺	☺	☺	☺	☺
Are there many code or regulatory requirements?	☺	☺	☺	☺	☺
Will this type project test our insurance liability limits?	☺	☺	☺	☺	☺
Questions About Client					
Have we worked with this client on other assignments?	☺	☺	☺	☺	☺
If so, did we have a sucessful relationship?	☺	☺	☺	☺	☺
If so, is the client a good reference?	☺	☺	☺	☺	☺
Did the client like to party?	☺	☺	☺	☺	☺
Is this a "hands-on client" ?	☺	☺	☺	☺	☺
Is this a "hands-off client" ?	☺	☺	☺	☺	☺
Is this an experienced client ?	☺	☺	☺	☺	☺
Will the senior management team be involved?	☺	☺	☺	☺	☺
Do we know others who have worked with the client?	☺	☺	☺	☺	☺
Does the client have a history of being litigious?	☺	☺	☺	☺	☺
Will our staff mesh well with this type client?	☺	☺	☺	☺	☺

Try to read the RFP as soon as you receive it to see if they are asking for things that will be time-consuming and that will involve others in preparation such as sketches, test layouts, building comparison statistics, or MEP and other consultants' proposals and fees.

PRESENTATIONS

As I mentioned in the RFP section, it is easier to make a pitch after receiving the RFP because you may have discovered something about the company or project that will help you differentiate yourself.

Having made many presentations, I still do not know when it seems best to present: first, middle, or last. I guess I prefer last for the reason that they will be ready with more good questions, and if the presentation is going well, it can run over. Often, the first presentation will not start on time, the middle one gets pinched for time so they can catch up, and by the third, the client is a bit relaxed and knows the important questions to ask.

It is only during your presentation that you have a real opportunity to set yourself apart from others. Proposals can look different and will have their own personality, but only in person can you easily show how you really think.

There are thirteen things to consider when making a presentation. (Sorry there are so many!)

THE BASICS

1. Preparation
Before you go to a presentation, you should find out:

- How much time will you have to present? The allotted time might seem quite short.
- Where it is going to be? Make sure you know the correct location and floor, and leave time to get through building security and maybe even client security.
- Who will be attending? What are their names and titles?
- What kind of a room is it? Is it an interior or exterior? Does it have glass walls? What kind of technology is available? Can the lights dim? If you think they might be open to having the presentation at your office rather than theirs, suggest that they could get introduced to the entire team and see your office in working mode.

2. Type of Assignment
Based on the type of assignment and location, do your research to determine:

- If you have done similar work—when, for whom, size, cost, realtor, contractor, and furniture. Try to get some matches going.
- Research everything you can about the company—products, services, stock price, number of offices, management team.

Where has the management team worked previously, and what schools did they attend?

- Ask if they will let you visit their existing office. If they will, make mental notes about office size, stations, furniture quality and manufacturer, density, amenities, colors and materials, and branding. It is also good to see the room you will be presenting in and look at the seating arrangement. It is most important to chat with them for a few minutes, so when you go to the presentation they know you.
- If you know the building or buildings they are considering, visit each one and make notes, take pictures, get plans, and maybe even do some type of test fit. They love that.

3. Format/Agenda

- Think about the type of presentation you want to make: 11 x 17 page-turner, formal PowerPoint, 24 x 36 boards on easels, bound presentation in 24 x 36 format as if it were a set of plans for a working meeting. Remember, if you are going to use boards, put the easels together in the office before you leave to make sure all the parts are included.
- It is very difficult to engage clients in a PowerPoint presentation in a room where the lights need to be dimmed or turned off. Clients are tired in the afternoon and sometimes even in the morning, if you are the third group they will see.

If you present in the afternoon, you might bring a little sherbet for them to have while you set up. Bring along some paper cups and spoons so you have everything you need. The sugar will pep them up for your presentation—and make them sleepy for the next one. We recently made a presentation where we all wore red buttons with different numbers on them. Finally, one of the clients said, "OK, what are the buttons all about?" I answered that the numbers represent the number of years each of us has been with the firm. In this case, we brought a senior team, so the numbers were very impressive. The numbers could have easily been the number of projects we did that were similar to theirs. *Do something special,* but not cute.

- Also with a PowerPoint presentation, if the lights are dimmed, it may be difficult for more than one on your team to talk.
- Prepare a draft outline of the agenda before you start pulling materials together. Do you have some special material to show that is directly applicable to what they are going to do? If so, start with that. Prepare a storyboard of how you want the presentation to go and who you want to do the talking.
- Know your audience. This is extremely important. Make sure you have something to discuss or show for everyone attending your presentation from the clients' team, including any outside consultants such as the realtor or owner's rep. The types of folks who typically come are: the CEO, COO, CFO, real estate agent, facilities manager, marketing team, administration, finance advisor, purchasing advisor, and human resources. HR folks are important because you can talk about how your great designs attract and retain staff, reduce churn, and minimize future hiring costs.
- As you prepare your presentation and discuss what you want to show, think about the appropriate person to focus on when you talk about that subject.
- The order in which you present your material depends a lot on how much information you were given. Remember, talk as much as you can about *them* and only reference your firm when appropriate. Do not go through your presentation in a boring chronological order with history, staff, and then the project phases. Try starting the presentation by talking about how successful the employee move-in went, and then lead into your services and the process that supported the tasks.

When you talk about the phases of work, it's best if you can talk about what you do differently in each phase, how your forms are better, and how the client benefits. If you are the second or third presenter, the client does not want to hear about the steps again; they are looking for differentiation. For instance, when I talked about managing the budget, I showed how our form was very different and made it much easier for the client to understand budget changes throughout the phases. The client could see *on one page* how scope changes affected the budget. It showed them that we wanted to be accountable.

When we talk about managing the schedule, we focus on the client's tasks, such as when we need their participation in each phase for planning, review, presentations, and approvals. Clients really do not care how you schedule your tasks. They need to know how to schedule their time with you.

4. Practice, Practice, Practice

Do a few practice runs with the team. Time your presentation. It will definitely pay off. Practice to stay within the allotted time so you don't have to rush through some of your most important information at the end when they say you have only five minutes left. Talk about the important topics first, and then, if you run out of time, you can say that the remaining material is in the copies that you will be leaving behind.

Emphasize how you are different or why working differently will benefit them. Leave time for questions; 10–15 minutes may be appropriate for a straightforward project.

5. Timing

Get there early—if you are not 15 minutes early, then you will probably be late. Being early is especially important if you are second or third, since there will be little time for you to set up. One of your team members should be chatting with the client and keeping them occupied during your setup. Being early is especially beneficial if you are first because you may get more time to present.

6. Your Opening

Which and how many employees you should bring depends on the type of project. As a rule, do not bring anyone who does not have something import-ant to contribute and do not bring more people than the client will have.

Introduce your team; name badges for your group work well. Set out a clear agenda that spells out what you are going to discuss. Remember, most people have a capacity for remembering three things. A well-known proponent of the "rule of three," Apple's Steve Jobs always said, "What are the three things you want them to remember?"

- The longer you take introducing your team, the less time you have to present. So succinctly introduce each one and say how they will be involved in your pitch.

- I find it is a good idea to design an agenda card. It's one piece of paper instead of a handful of business cards that they will surely lose right after the meeting. With your photos on the card, they will more easily connect the faces with what was said when they are chatting about your firm after the presentation. They can also make a few notes on the card when you say something brilliant.
- Be aware of the seating arrangement. It is usually easy to figure out where the head person is going to sit. Do not sit there. Have your team sit more in the back, away from the door but where you all can talk to the client. Put your briefcases, notebooks, etc., out of the way to reduce clutter.
- If you plan to use a computer or projector, bring all your connections and a few extension cords, in case there aren't enough outlets in the conference room.

Front and back of card

7. The Client's Team

It is important to know who is coming to your presentation from your client's team. Your client's team may also include consultants they may have already retained. It is *imperative* that your presentations include something for everyone. It is especially important that you understand what role each person will play, so your presentation includes subjects that they will be interested in. If they do not have business cards, write down their information so you can send each of them a thank-you note after the presentation. Typically, the client does not bring business cards when the meeting is in their office.

The following list details some of the things we like to discuss with the client. Pick one or two positive points to discuss with each of the client representatives.

CEO/COO

- Review of things learned from the website or articles
- Growth of stock price, if relevant
- Revenue growth of company—past five years—if relevant
- Projected growth over next five years—if relevant
- Reason for expanding/relocating/building
- On move-in day, what would he/she like to say to employees?
  - Project goals—new ways of working
  - Space efficiency
  - Building amenities
  - Environmental controls; green materials
  - Ecology
  - Planned new products
  - Image to be projected to clients

CFO/Purchasing

- Budget controls/Schedule controls
- Planned scope or quality options
- Bidding and accounting standards
- Contracts

CIO

- Internal technology systems
- External technology systems
- AV, IT, desktop security

Real Estate/Facilities Person

- Space standards
- Furniture standards
- Quality of materials
- Bidding procedures
- Selecting other consultants
- Lease/purchase review
- Projecting growth

HR

Coordinating workplace standards with Real estate/Facilities

Employee amenity program

Communication with employees during entire process

Communication with employees after move-in

8. Questions During the Presentation

I like to say the client can ask all the questions he or she wants during the presentation. You want their involvement. However, I am never sure how many questions we should ask. An important rule is to never ask a question unless you know they can and will answer it. You certainly don't want to embarrass anyone.

9. Questions You Cannot Answer

If the client asks a question and you do not have an immediate answer, that is OK, but keep in mind that not knowing an answer can be worse than giving a wrong answer. Buy yourself some time and follow this simple rule: If you do not know an answer, say you will get the information and send it to them the same or next day. Actually, this can be a positive thing because it is good to have a reason to continue a dialogue after the presentation.

If it is a question like "What is RSF?" and you do not know the answer, you may be in trouble. Often the questions that I do not have immediate answers to are about some of our past projects like cost/RSF, schedule, and things like that. Think twice before you give an answer. Perhaps the information should be kept confidential. Thinking about the question after the meeting gives you more time to prepare a good answer, and this avoids giving a rushed answer. If you send the answer in an email, do not forget to copy everyone who was at the meeting.

10. Tricky Questions You Might Be Asked

When you are showing examples of your work, the client may ask, "How much did that project cost?" You should bring a project metrics card for each project you show. If you do, you will look super organized and experienced and be able to thoroughly answer the question. You should also have a back-up sheet describing what makes up the costs of a project to show how each is so different.

Many times there cannot be an answer because either the site has not been selected, a personnel and space program not developed, or a design even started. Some tricky questions you might be asked include:

- How much do you think we need to budget for this project?
- How much space do you think we will need to lease?
- How long will the project take from start to finish?
- What are the risks we will have working with your company?

These are "no-win" questions. The best you can do is to give ranges, be brief, and hope for the best.

11. Timing

Never watch the clock. You should know how long your presentation will take. Do not say, "We're almost out of time so I'll rush through the photos"; rather, say, "We did not show all the photos. You'll find the rest in the booklet we are leaving with you." Summarize your three-point presentation emphasizing your strengths, your desire to work with them, and your commitment to quality and success.

12. Regroup and Follow Up

When the team is back in the office, get together to discuss how the presentation went and talk about improvements to be made for next time. Refer to the checklist to determine whether you followed your plan.

Write a letter or email to the client to address any lingering questions or concerns. Say "thank you" in this letter, and send it to all those who attended the presentation. If you want to send a separate "thank-you" card to add a personal touch, send a nice one to everyone who attended the presentation.

13. Finding Out Their Decision

Accepted

Congratulations! Party time!

Rejected

First, I would send a nice card or note and say, 'If for any reason it does not work out with the chosen firm, we are very eager to come aboard."

Second, there are times when the contract with the other firm is not signed, so you want them to know you are ready to chat. Over the years, there were a few times I was so upset we did not get the project that I went on a *polite* campaign to continue presenting our case. I called anyone I could restating our case and sending them additional photos and materials, and then one day the client called and said we got the job!

Third, *do not give up.* Be polite and never speak disrespectfully of the selected firm.

Here are a few general facts about projects:

- The smaller the project, the greater the cost per square foot
- The greater the number of offices vs. open workstations, the greater the base cost of construction will be.
- Projects costs vary considerably depending on IT, security, AV equipment, telephone costs, generator, UPS, furniture, level of finish, building owner contribution, free rent allocated to work, etc.
- Occupancy metrics are also easy to be misunderstood. Companies occupying similar square footage can have very different USF/person and RSF/person numbers depending on workplace standards and types of special areas. One company may have special areas such as large rooms for training, a cafeteria, a fitness center, and storage. These skew the SF/person numbers.

CHAPTER 9

You Got the Project

WHAT IS YOUR FIRM'S ROLE?

Even after you have made your presentation and submitted your proposal, and the client says your firm is selected, there are a number of questions that may still need to be cleared up. It is important to ask what others, PM or owner's rep, are or will be contracted for. Try to ask about services that may be duplicated.

Here are a few areas of overlap:

Project Manager/Owner's Rep

The client may have selected a firm or plans to hire a firm to manage the project. Often the client does not have the experience in-house and will solicit proposals for this service. Most of the time, these firms will have been selected before the architect, and, if so, they will write your RFP. If not, the architect can assist in writing the RFP for their work.

Budget and Schedule

It needs to be clear in the contract who is going to prepare and maintain the master schedule and the budget.

Preparing RFPs (Interviewing, and Recommending the Remaining Consultants)

Who is going to be doing these tasks for such positions as MEP, civil, construction manager, acoustical, security, IT, lighting, etc.?

Preparing Bid Packages, Soliciting Bids, Leveling Bids, and Recommending Firms

Who will be charge of these tasks for furniture, security, audio visual, and construction?

There is a lot of time and effort that needs to be expended to carry out each of the tasks listed above. If these services are within the architect's scope, then the contract and fee needs to be clear and reflected in the total scope. If these services are the responsibilities of others, but it is suggested or required that the architect "assist" others, then you *must* account for the time and make sure there is an appropriate fee included. Even if the architect is not responsible, time will surely be expended.

FINALIZING YOUR ARCHITECTURAL CONTRACT

The next step is preparing a written contract with your new client. We always prefer the client to sign *our* proposal or contract because the scope of work is clearly set out. If the client has an owner's rep or project manager on board, they will still want their attorney to be involved. Be prepared to spend some time getting the contract finalized.

Try to do the negotiations *in person* with the attorney and the client who will eventually sign off on your contract. Remember that attorneys charge by the hour; if possible, avoid email negotiations that usually take forever.

In all contracts there are different points:

1. **Points you can agree to immediately**
   My approach is to start with all the points you can agree to without any changes. This is a positive start to your contract negotiations, and it sets a proper tone and shows willingness to be cooperative.
2. **Scope issues that need to be settled or modified**
   Next, I try to get all the issues of scope: work to be included, work to be excluded, and work where the architect's role is to assist others, properly documented.
3. **Language that you cannot live with—deal breakers**
   Points you cannot agree to, as written, I call *deal breakers*. They will take the longest to negotiate and are the most important to resolve. These are often clauses making the architect responsible for things out of his or her control, such as cost overruns or schedule slippage. These clauses may also include severe penalties if these situations occur.

Some contracts say that if the project costs do not come in within budget, the architect will recommend changes and redraw at their cost to bring the costs in line with the budget. The language *should* say that if the architectural portion of the budget comes in over the estimated architectural cost, the architect will evaluate alternatives, recommend changes, and, if necessary, make appropriate plan revisions at their expense. What is important is that the other consulting firms, such as MEP, IT, AV, security, acoustical, and lighting, need to agree to the same language in their contracts and be responsible for their own work and budgets.

4. Clauses where your liability insurance policy does not cover you

I always leave the liability points for last. If the clauses in the contract do not align with the limits or language in the architect's liability policy, or are unusually restrictive, I will say, "Our liability carrier does not cover architects for these words or clauses. If you want the highlighted clauses to stay in the contract, we will prepare a disclaimer saying we are signing the document as is but please note our insurance carrier does not cover us for these clauses." Most of the time, the disclaimer approach works to notify the client. If the proposed limits of liability are higher than we carry, we will tell the client how much our carrier will charge for the increased coverage and treat it as an extra.

5. Fee negotiations

After time is spent discussing each point with the negotiator(s) to get the contract as fair as possible for both the client and the architect, sometimes the negotiator still wants the last ounce of blood from the architect. They ask you to drop your fee. It is very tough to make a blanket recommendation to you about what to do in this situation. When it happens to me, I present my case from four points of view. I will say to the negotiator or client:

- I bid very tight on the RFP because we really want to do this project with the client.
- The scope is not completely defined and we have made some allowances in our timing, so we will not come back and "nickel-and-dime you."

- The architectural percentage of the "fee pie" is a very small percentage of total fees, usually around 13 percent, and a very small percent of total costs.
- Our goal is to design a project that meets the client's goals and objectives for the least possible cost. We also help negotiate the fees of the MEP, lighting and acoustical engineers, the furniture dealer, and, most important, the contractor. That's where there will be considerable savings.

I think it is important for the client to understand how their money is spent. The percentages of the "fee pie," as indicated in the following example, demonstrates just how much actually goes to each consultant, based on an average architectural interior project of 50,000 RSF.

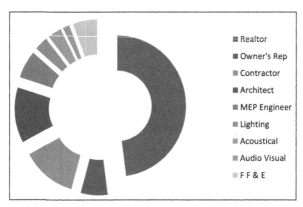

Where the money goes.

Even though the real estate fee is not paid directly by the client to the realtor, it is included as part of the base rent the client is paying.

Be organized when presenting your case in any negotiation. Keep in mind that the client selected you and wants to work with your firm, so do not be unreasonable with your demands. Once your contract is approved, the other consultants' contracts should be easy to finalize.

BUILDING THE EXTERNAL TEAM

Part of the architect's scope may be to select the other project consultants. This may include sending out RFPs, interviewing, leveling bids, and making recommendations to the client. This is a very time-consuming task and needs to be well organized and done quickly to get the other firms on board before the project is too far down the road.

Three things are important to know when negotiating consultants' contracts:

1. Who has the final approval of the recommended firms?
2. Who will the firms be contracted with?
3. How are they to be paid? What is the invoice approval process?

I recommend the client attend the interviews with the key consulting groups, like the project manager, the MEP engineers, and the construction manager, if there is one. I recommend that contracts be held by the client and that the invoices be reviewed by the architect and paid by the client. It is critical that each consultant understand and agree to the terms in the architect's contract with the client. The architect's contract may have specifics about process, payments, timing, additional services, and changes to approved scope, budget, and liability.

As the business changes, so must the contracts and the way services are delivered, especially the way services are invoiced. The following billing schedule by phase is prepared in two columns: the first shows "historical" project percentages and the second column, "current," shows how we are shifting the fee more to the beginning of the project where the costs of staff are considerably higher:

Project Invoicing by Phase

	Historical	Current
Prelease		
Envisioning	inc	5%
Site Selection	inc	5%
Programming	5%	5%
Test Fits	inc	5%
Schematic Design	20%	30%
Design Development	15%	10%
Furniture Specifications	additional	hourly or fixed
Construction Documents	40%	25%
Bidding	inc	inc
Construction Observation	20%	15%
Punch List		inc
Move-In		inc
Close-Out		inc
	100%	100%

In Part IV, I outlined some of the things to think about when an employee moves up to a management role. Finding new opportunities for the firm is very difficult and requires a tremendous amount of creativity. For each new project, there are probably a number of potential opportunities that do not materialize. At first, the marketing responsibility will feel like a second job assisting the principal(s) in review of RFPs, proposal writing, and preparation of presentations.

PART V

Reassessing Your Career

CHAPTER 10

Should I Stay or Should I Go?

EVALUATION: ASKING FOR A RAISE OR MOVING ON

Writing about the best way to ask for a review and presumably a raise or knowing when it's time to start looking for a new job is difficult because everyone's situation is different.

To make it easier, let's look at the two questions separately.

First, let's discuss the question of the *raise*. There are a number of factors:

1. When you joined the firm, did you discuss having an annual review? Is it in writing in your letter of understanding? If it is, and the firm said they give annual reviews and your year is up, then you should ask for one. I presume for this exercise you are doing well, probably doing more than is expected, and the quality of your work is high. I am also presuming the person that you will ask for the review is aware of your day-to-day work and understands firsthand your contribution. If the person you meet with does not have firsthand knowledge of your situation, you can either ask your direct manager to be in the meeting or prepare notes that can be reviewed later with others.

2. Before you ask for the raise, make notes for yourself about the work you are doing, especially if you are working at a higher level with more responsibility than expected. Also, make notes about any "extra effort" projects you did individually or with others. The bottom line is to be prepared.

3. If you got a great review but no raise was offered, then you need to know the reasons. If the economy is bad or if the office is not doing well, that is not your fault. Perhaps in those cases a cost of living increase is appropriate. If the money is not there to give you a raise, perhaps you can suggest greater benefits, such as more time off, a new title, better insurance coverage, etc.

4. If you are put off, then you need to ask why. You may not like the answer, but it is always better to know if the firm does not think you are doing well than to continue to work under those conditions.

5. If you see contemporaries being promoted and you are not getting the recognition you think you deserve, then it is appropriate to ask for a review. Every office has a pace, a level of pressure and stress and depending on your role; you can feel whether the firm is doing well.

6. You can tell by the mood of the principals, the number of closed-door meetings, and the number of new projects. Everyone senses trouble whether individually or as a group. There are no secrets in an architectural office.

7. If you did not get a raise or a cost of living increase but you understood the comments made about your performance and you agree that there is potential in your future, then stick it out and work your hardest. However, if you didn't get a raise or a cost of living increase and you were not happy with the review, it may make sense to start updating your portfolio and your résumé and start looking for another job.

UPDATING YOUR PORTFOLIO AND RÉSUMÉ AND PREPARING FOR INTERVIEWS

Second, let's discuss what to do if you decide it is time to move on. It takes a lot of discipline to keep track of people whom you have met and who can help you in situations like this. I have seen many interns and architects keep a running list of their personal and professional contacts by discipline. Knowing whom to call when you need a quick reference or recommendation is important.

Always ask a person if you can use his or her name as a reference when looking for a new job. Ask whether they are willing to take a call to discuss your capabilities. You can do this each time or get a blanket approval and use it anytime.

You should be able to add to the portfolio you used when applying for the job you have now. Always show your freshest work first in a portfolio. All employees, whether their employers think so or not, keep plans and photos of their existing work just for this purpose—portfolio updates. In addition to plans and photos of projects you worked on, develop a metrics fact sheet for each project. It is embarrassing when an interviewer asks how large a project is or what the exterior material was or whose windows you used and you have a blank look on your face. The interviewer may interpret your lack of knowledge as not having worked on the project.

On the fact sheet, make a statement of exactly what you did, including all your tasks and responsibilities, so it is clear to the interviewer. If you write this information in the same format as your résumé, it becomes very easy to keep everything up-to-date. Even though you now have more experience than when you first applied for a job, still keep your résumé to one page. CVs can be much longer, but I do not believe they are necessary for the average architectural interview.

CHAPTER 12

Taking the Plunge to Start Your Own Firm

To those of you planning to start your own architectural or interior design firm, *think about the way you want others to think of you and your services* as a leader, an expert, or an authority. This is so that when you are marketing yourself for a potential assignment, you present from a position of strength rather than from the position of sales.

In architecture, not everyone can be an expert in design and present themselves with award-winning projects. But you can be extremely knowledgeable about the architectural process, about getting projects done on time and within budget, or as a subject matter expert on design specialties such as schools, hospitals, or residential structures.

Clients can see salespeople coming a mile away, and like most of us, they are reluctant to trust them. On the other hand, when one is considered a leader or authority on a subject because of what he or she has built, written, or taught, we look forward to hearing what they have to say.

We hope all clients buy relationships and not price or product. I encourage you to use ideas in this section and Section 5 to show your firm's project potential and employee capabilities from the strongest point of view.

STARTING WITH A BLANK CANVAS

People often say, "If I'd known how long it would take or how much it would cost, I never would have started." Thinking back about starting CPG Architects in 1980, I would do it again in a heartbeat even though I had no idea what I was getting into. However, having a book like this with suggestions on how to organize my thoughts, my office, and my strengths would have been invaluable to me.

Like many others, I started without the proper understanding of what would be involved, how long it would take, what it would cost, or how difficult it would be for my family. It was a gut reaction to a bad experience that fortunately worked out very well.

By late 1979, I knew my time at Amex was ending, based upon a number of bad experiences I was having with my boss. It was a Friday in November when he made it easy for me to leave. That evening, my wife and I were meeting friends at Dominic's in the Bronx, and no one knew of my situation. I was coming from the City by subway and meeting my wife and friends for a great Italian dinner. After we all sat down and ordered drinks, I announced I was no longer with Amex, and for some reason everyone cheered and congratulated me, ordered champagne, and toasted my newfound freedom. I did not realize how much I must have telegraphed my unhappiness working with this fellow.

Of course, the question asked was "What do you want to do next?" and I answered in a very cavalier way, "Start my own business."

That weekend I planned an approach, and on Monday I started chatting with friends, asking, "How do I do this?" and "What am I getting myself into?"

BEST ADVICE I GOT

When friends heard I was thinking about starting my own firm, there was no shortage of ideas and advice. Only a few had actually started their own businesses and none had started an architectural firm, so the advice was all over the map.

My best advice came from Michael Siegel, a broker with Cushman and Wakefield (C&W) in Stamford, Connecticut. American Express used C&W for real estate services in New York City, so getting access and a meeting with the head of their Stamford office was easy. He had a broad overview of the business, knew what kinds of services companies were looking for, and certainly knew my competition and their capabilities.

I was surprised by Michael's advice. What he said sounded so simple: understand what makes the different disciplines tick—especially your competitors—and most important, *find out how you can help others.* Michael said that I should not try to go out and find a project as quickly as I could, because I would get busy doing that work and miss the opportunity to meet others in the marketplace and find out how I compared to the competition.

What Michael did not say was how long I should do this. It's like your broker or a friend recommending a stock that goes up quickly, but they don't tell you when to get out.

What Michael said sounded so simple, but in reality, it was very hard. I thought, how do I find these contacts? How am I going to be introduced? Whom should I call first and what should I say if we get together? I thought, should I ask to come to their office, or meet them for breakfast or lunch? What should I show them about what I had been doing for American Express? Should I bring up my Caudill Rowlett Scott experience?

There are two ways most architects start their own business:

1. You can leave an architectural firm and take a few clients with you to pay the immediate bills while you establish your new credentials. When you start this way, at least you know the players in the marketplace and a bit about marketing, proposal writing, presentations, billing, and production.
2. When you start as I did with no contacts and not knowing anyone in the marketplace, the task became quite daunting, even though Michael's advice was so clear.

I needed to find a way to meet a number of very different types of compatible professionals as quickly as I could. It goes without saying that as a young person of 38 with two little kids and living in a house in Greenwich that was under renovation, I had not saved any money to start this business. This opportunity came suddenly, and the minor detail of not having any money proved very difficult. I also knew that "just meeting loads of people" was not going to help. I needed to meet people who could help me get started. I also knew that no one was going to help if he or she could not also benefit.

The idea I came up with was to start a networking group of professionals that consulted with corporations in all capacities.

I called the group ONE OF A KIND. That fit well with the initial name of my firm—The Corporate Planning Group. I thought the group should include one person from each of the following types of consulting companies:

- Real estate
- Engineering
- Construction
- Marketing
- Graphics
- Landscape
- Location consulting
- Acoustical
- Lighting
- Mover
- Developer
- Furniture dealer
- Telephone
- Security
- Attorney
- AV/Technology

It was not as hard as I thought getting the group together, because after I found the first person, each one recommended someone else. I did this before "lead/marketing groups" became fashionable.

The first few meetings were informative, and people shared a lot of knowledge about the marketplace, the players, and potential projects, knowing that it would not be broadcast to their competition. I made some very good long-term friends and contacts and even got a few leads and the opportunity to make presentations. I did not get any work out of the references; however, it was an excellent networking opportunity, and I was learning a lot in the process.

My first project actually came from a friend of my wife's, and that started me off. It was a branch office of a law firm in Stamford. It took six months to get that first job because, as hard as I tried, and as much experience as I thought I had, I did not have a track record of completed projects done by my new company. No one had heard of The Corporate Planning Group.

Eventually, I figured out what the realtors were looking for, what the clients wanted to hear, and how I needed to position our services to create value. We ended that first year working on 10 projects.

A DAUNTING NUMBER OF INTERRELATED TASKS-REFERENCES

Building a Project/Client Reference list is critical not only when you start your firm, but throughout the life of the business. Every time a project is finished, it is important to ask the client if they will be a reference, and if photos of their finished project (with or without their name) can be used in your marketing efforts.

 One thing most people forget in building a reference list is to include all the other consultants' names that worked on the project. For instance, when the attorney for the law firm said I could use their name as a reference, I also included the names of the realtor, engineer, contractor, and furniture dealer on the list. This is how I helped others get visibility, and this approach actually helped me get additional work.

MARKETING: CREATING A PORTFOLIO

Without good design, no one wants to hire your firm; without good project management, the firm would not get repeat business; and without financial controls in place to facilitate timely billing, the firm may go broke.

What I am saying is that you need to be well balanced in marketing all aspects of your company's business. Developing your marketing skills early in your career is the most important thing you can do personally to help yourself move up the ladder or to develop confidence if and when you decide to start your own firm.

All architectural and interiors firms have four prime areas of responsibility:

1. Marketing
2. Design
3. Project Management
4. Finance/Office Management

Most firms do three types of marketing:

1. Direct marketing includes:
   - Cold calling—picking up the phone to call someone you may or may not know
   - Writing a letter or sending an email to someone you do not know
   - Targeted mailings—mailing a specific marketing piece to someone who is not expecting it

Keep in mind that the response rate for direct marketing is below 1 percent unless the subject you are marketing is a very hot topic.

2. Indirect marketing includes:
   - Social media including a website, Facebook, LinkedIn, Twitter, Snapchat, or Instagram
   - Articles written by individuals in the firm
   - A firm blog including case studies of projects
   - Parties for clients and vendors (don't forget the vendors)
   - Speaking engagements
   - Joining networking or community groups
   - Participating in volunteer activities

The response rate for indirect marketing is probably 1–2 percent unless the subject is very specific and you send out emails noting you have a new post or will do something in the future.

3. Direct help (the best approach in the long run):
   - Giving direct help to someone who gets an assignment
   - Saying nice things about someone to others
   - Telling someone about an opportunity that turns into a project
   - Helping a person who is out of work get an interview or, better yet, a job
   - Referring a company for a new assignment that they get

When you use direct help as a major focus of your marketing strategy, the response rate can be the highest.

Portfolio

Your portfolio needs two distinct parts:

- Part 1 describes who you are, including your firm's goals, objectives, services offered, project approach, processes, client references, etc. Do not forget to ask for references from team members on projects you worked on together.
- Part 2 describes what you have done. In my situation, this was minimal for the first year or so.

I found that clients wanted to hear about both. Fortunately, my story about who I was, what I did at Amex, and my understanding of what the corporate client was looking for helped me get a number of jobs, even though my "What I Have Done" portfolio was very lean. Including the other team players on my project/client list was a real benefit. First, it made the list look larger; second, the potential client would often know one or more of the others and by default, it gave me credibility. Giving credit to the entire team benefits all.

Administrative Processes

Having to come up with the best ways to do simple things like getting out letters, mailing, copying, printing hand drawings, using delivery services, paying bills, keeping track of expenses, and preparing marketing materials was daunting. Working 80 or more hours a week was the norm. I tried to spend each day working with clients, working on projects, and doing marketing. Nights and weekends were reserved for office management tasks and drawing.

I think back to those busy days without mobile phones, computers, Word, Excel, PowerPoint, Printers, FedEx, Fax, or a myriad of other business tools we now take for granted. Presentations were paste-ups, and then a rush to a printer to have a photostat made for a meeting the next morning. I made a number of presentations like those that we did at Caudill Rowlett Scott—on rolls of brown paper. These were great-looking, made a major impact, were quick to do, and did not require reproduction. The downside was they were impossible to modify when you made a mistake.

Leveraging Past Experiences

As I wrote in Part I, each of your experiences, even those summer jobs you had, matters. Each experience builds on the other to make up *your story*. My corporate experience, working for a large company like American Express, which had 3,500 locations in 125 countries, was exhilarating. There were no two days alike, no two experiences alike, and no two people alike. The amount you can learn is directly related to the effort you want to exert. Perhaps it should be a requirement that everyone apprenticing in our business work for a corporation in a real estate, facility management, or design capacity to experience firsthand the information a corporate person needs to have to manage their work and to be able to respond to others internally in a timely fashion.

"Co-Opetition"

Co-Opetition is the name of a great book by Adam Brandenburger and Barry Nalebuff. It is a must-read for architects.

"Co-opetition" is a term used to describe service professionals who sometimes cooperate with one another in their quest for new business or other times compete with one another for that new business. As allied professionals add to their service offerings, it is logical that many of these companies will provide similar services. In the architectural world, we frequently see architects compete for assignments against a developer who brings an architect on his team or a design/build firm that has an in-house architect. In the interior design business, real estate companies and furniture manufactures/dealers sometimes coordinate their efforts to go after projects, and other times these firms compete for parts of the same projects.

Here is a brief excerpt from *Co-Opetition*:

> A player is your **complementor** if customers value your product more when they have the other player's product than when they have your

product alone. A player is your **competitor** if customers value your product less when they have the other player's product than when they have your product alone. Many people simply assume the rules of business—both formal and informal—are set in stone and are not subject to negotiation. That is incorrect. There is no reason why you should blindly follow the rules—you can change them at any time. Keep in mind that works both ways. At any time, your competitors, suppliers or competitors can change the rules as well. They do not necessarily have to follow the same rules as you do. In the marketplace, whichever party has the power gets to make the rules.[3]

Branding the Business

Branding needs to start the day you hang up your shingle. Your business card, logo, and marketing materials must clearly represent who you are. This is part of your brand.

When it comes to your brand, the visual and tangible things you do are important, but the intangibles, such as the way you treat others and the way you thank others, make a more lasting impression. Our websites, Facebook, and LinkedIn pages talk about who we are as well as the things we do for others, like the nonprofits we contribute to and the helpful activities all our staff does every week. This shows what we stand for. Put your time and efforts into community activities. These efforts go a long way and are rarely forgotten by your contacts and clients. Keep your social media sites up-to-date with photo shoots, award submissions, newsletter or blog ideas, special events, or speaking engagements.

Branding Your Employees

In a service business, a company's employees are its most valuable asset. Second is the company's "brand." Your brand is what differentiates your company from others because it is a promise of trust, and quality delivered through your employees, whom I will call your "brand ambassadors." These brand ambassadors represent the company in everything they do when working on projects, presenting themselves in social media, and doing community work. The hope each firm has is that these ambassadors clearly understand the message the company wants to express about its products and services.

---

3 Adam M. Brandenburger and Barry J. Nalebuff, *Co-Opetition*, Currency Doubleday, 1997.

Your company should encourage and support employees' personal activities, whether it's fundraising such as cancer runs and walks, building homes through Habitat for Humanity, or volunteering at the local soup kitchen. Buying the shirts and hats for an event or a team shows the firm supports its staff.

Market research shows that companies with engaged employees have:

- 51% lower turnover
- 18% more productivity
- 12% higher profitability
- 27% less absenteeism

Here are a few ideas we have found that work well at our company to coordinate brand awareness:

- *Include all employees in company successes.* Celebrate victories and recognize those who helped the company accomplish its goals.
- *Hire people who love the company brand.* Hiring the right people from the start ensures that employees continue to share the correct brand story. Hire people who believe in your company values and want to be a part of your brand's story.
- *Differentiate.* Every business decision should have differentiation top of mind. Challenge the competition.
- *Make company values a priority.* All employees should embody your company's culture and values such as caring, integrity, passion, and fun.

THE IMPORTANCE OF METRICS

When you are starting out, it is easy to remember the facts about each client, each project, team members, fees, etc. As you grow and have a few more employees, it is critical for you to have a way to access project facts quickly.

This is especially true when responding to an RFP. Many of the questions in an RFP or RFI refer to:

- The number, size, and costs of projects of a certain type
- The location and year in which each was completed

- Final costs for base building vs. interior development
- Special amenity features of each
- Project team list/other consultants
- Prime contractor and subcontractors
- Client references

Keeping these facts in a program and in a format easy to copy into the RFP saves a lot of time. An RFP template should include all the important questions asked along with your standard answers. Many of the questions asked in an RFI/RFP are similar.

The first thing to do is look for questions you have *not* been asked before and add them to the template. When it comes time to prepare the RFP, it is just a matter of cut and paste. *Do not cut and paste without reading the question and your answers carefully.* You may be embarrassed by including an inappropriate answer.

Another reason to keep metrics organized is for quick reference to the number of hours spent on a project. Time spent by person and per phase should give you an idea how to position your fee, especially if you also track project profitability.

Metrics are also important to help the team remember facts about prior projects. For example:

- Remembering the utilization of space—USF or RSF per person for similar project types
- Knowing which furniture manufacturer was used on a prior project and the cost per USF, cost per person, or cost per configuration
- Remembering significant materials used such as curtain walls, windows, flooring, ceilings, and hardware helps when designing a new project

It is also important for the staff to know which consultants were used on prior projects. Be aware of the number of projects given to each consulting firm. When possible, spread the business around so you have a larger base that can potentially refer your firm. There are metrics you might want to keep a little more private:

- Revenue per month per year—track against last year
- Revenue per employee per month

- Expenses per month
- Project profitability (know which projects to watch more closely)
- Project by phase (know if any projects are behind schedule)
- Backlog—by type and size
- Receivables and cash on hand

Knowing your metrics is also important when meeting informally with potential clients or friends who are in a position to recommend your firm. Having information readily available is critical to being able to manage efficiently. Keeping project photos on your phone or tablet is also useful because when someone talks about an idea, you can email a photo to them right away.

It is all about being ready all of the time.

REPEAT BUSINESS VS. NEW BUSINESS

Repeat business is the best business we have, and I have always performed with that hope in mind. We have over 75 percent repeat clients each year, and, after a while, it feels like you are working with family and that feels good. I think everyone knows the positives of having repeat business, but let me list a few of the benefits:

- It takes far fewer marketing dollars to secure a new client
- Processes and procedures are known, thus reducing the learning curve
- Expectations are understood
- Friendships continue

On the negative side (yes, there can be negatives):

- Repeat projects often result in lower fees per SF or negotiated contracts
- Clients often ask to work with the same team members even if they may be deeply involved in other work
- Team members can get burned out when they work on repetitive projects
- Significant repeat business can result in reduced marketing efforts to find new clients—40 percent repeat business is a good target

Being called back for repeat business is due primarily to the firm's great service and design efforts. Firms should not get complacent and forget they must continually elevate the quality of the relationship by:

- Keeping the client abreast of key industry developments, trending design concepts, and new technologies. Firms need to understand the difference between being a great vendor and a strategic partner. Strategic partners keep their client's program issues on the front burner with articles on the latest thinking.
- Sharing case studies, best practices, and new ideas that promote facility management applications, work order integration, and green initiatives.

DISRUPT OR BE DISRUPTED

In an earlier chapter, I talked about the way individuals can be disruptors in the firm by doing more than was anticipated. This section contains ideas about how the firm can do more to be noticed and stay in front of the competition.

One of the first things each new owner has to do when he or she starts a new business is to put together a marketing package. An important part of the package will be a list of the services you plan on providing. Often lists are alphabetized on websites, missing the opportunity to show additional benefits. These are a few organizational ideas that will be more interesting to your clients.

Your services could be organized by:

- Phase provided: PL, SD, DD, CD, CA, Move-in, Close-Out
- Type of project—architectural vs. interior
- Services designed to save money or time
- Services that increase efficiency, flexibility, or collaboration
- Services that enhance your client's brand

Be a disruptor—provide innovative services that are performed after the main project is complete. There are a number of subscription-type services you can bill monthly, which extends your cash flow well beyond the end of the project.

Identify services that you can provide in collaboration with others.

When you compare traditional architectural services to those provided by the top real estate companies, you will see overlap in many areas. The same holds true when you review the services offered by many of the top furniture manufacturers/dealers. Approach these firms and offer to joint-venture on some services. If they say yes, at least you will be getting part of the fee for the service instead of letting them take it all.

Here is how some furniture manufacturers advertise their services:

Our Design Services Are Complimentary

You bring your budget and goals, and we will help you do the rest. Our full suite of services will help you through every step of the process, from project management and space planning to delivery and installation. Best of all, these services are at *no cost to you*. It's a complimentary service as part of your furniture purchase.

It is very hard to compete against a free service.

The same holds true for real estate firms. Many offer similar services as incentives to the client if they are selected to provide lease/buy/sell activities.

They perform nonliability services such as:

- Consultant selection, bidding, and contract negotiations
- Building comparisons
- Building/system analysis
- Programming and space forecasting
- Workplace strategy
- Project management
- Preconstruction pricing and bidding
- Furniture bidding and procurement
- Project close-out
- Lease management
- Facility management

Architects should be providing these profitable services.

The nonliability type services listed above can be easily separated from the traditional "heavy liability" architectural services such as preparation of construction documents, bidding, and specifications.

So what can and should architects do to offset the loss of services and income?

1. Continue to include additional profitable services in your proposal as a basic service or as an extra service
2. Start to offer Day 2 services to stay in contact with the client. These are described in Chapter 7: Day 2 Services
3. Learn to joint-venture with the real estate firm. They probably do not have the in-house capabilities and will need to joint-venture with someone—why not you?

MENTORING

Every office should set up a mentoring program for employees to have coworkers to bounce ideas off of, check their work, and learn new technical tricks.

The role of the original mentor will diminish as the employee gains more experience and a new mentor, offering another level or type of experience, may take over. Mentoring is by far the best and fastest way for staff to grow. Remember, mentoring is a two-way street—either you are a mentor or you are being mentored. Mentoring should not be thought of as "supervising," although both give helpful advice. Mentoring is more like "developing." Some companies consider those who help others with specific functions or tasks as an add-on to their job description. The role of the boss used to be more hands-off. Now firms consider it a boss's responsibility to be actively involved with employees' career goals and professional development. In order to be a mentor or a boss who cares, it is important to reexamine how you manage your time to be available to others. One of the top reasons a person voluntarily leaves a firm is a bad boss.

We require all employees to read the contracts for projects they are working on and read all the correspondence going out and coming in. It is the best way to know what is happening, but also to learn about the big picture.

THINK 360

Architects who have worked in a facility management capacity in a corporate real estate department know exactly how hard it is to manage day-to-day change after an "out of the ground" or interiors project is completed. It is tough when the consulting teams have moved on to other projects and are not available to make small changes.

Most architects focus on the main project, and few are concerned with or even interested in developing applications to assist corporations on a daily basis with the little things. Architects are waiting for the next large project.

Therefore, Day 2 work can be very beneficial to your firm from a number of points of view:

- First of all, the work is usually on an hourly or contract basis with no discounting—no bidding required.
- Second, you can establish a much longer-term relationship with the client and move yourself into a position of helping on other properties. Converting a vendor/consultant relationship into a strategic partner relationship comes with many benefits.
- Third, you will know when the next project is coming along and hopefully be in a position to get the work without competitive bidding.
- Fourth, Day 2 work can turn into subscription services rather than fee-based services and continue for years.
- Fifth, ongoing Day 2 services smooth out the highs and lows of a traditional architectural practice from a staff as well as a financial point of view.

The negative side to Day 2 work is that many architects only want to work on new assignments and not rehash completed projects. Frankly, some actually look down on doing moves or adds and changes. *Facility management* is not a positive phrase for the architect who studied design for five or six years in architecture school. This is just one more "real world" lesson you do not learn in school.

CPG Architects is a perfect case study. I started CPG Architects in 1980, providing architectural and interior design services to corporations in the New York, New Jersey, and Connecticut market. For the first 10 or so years, everything was manual: drawing, typing, calculating, and so forth.

As I stated in the section on American Express in a previous chapter, I always wanted to design a computer system based on what I needed at American Express. It would enable our clients to easily track and report on space, people, furniture, and equipment changes. When you are on staff, it is necessary to be able to answer management's questions in a timely fashion.

In the early 90s, instead of buying a PC with AutoCAD, we bought a Mac with a large radius monitor and a program called Aperture. Aperture is a drawing application that enables the user to prepare drawings, create and attach records to a drawing object, and then report on the data.

There was no programming involved, so the flexibility to create applications was endless. For years, we used Aperture to do all the firm's project drawings, including CDs. At the end of the assignment, the plans were ready to sell a facility management service. Thinking 360 was natural based on my prior experience.

The difficulty turned out to be that companies did not want to buy computer services from an architectural firm. We solved that problem by creating a real estate software subsidiary called Link Systems, a separate company organized to design, service, and sell lease management, facility management, and portfolio management applications.

Instead of thinking in a traditional linear way—get the job, do it, and wait to be invited to help on the next job—firms need to think creatively about providing additional services after the main project is completed.

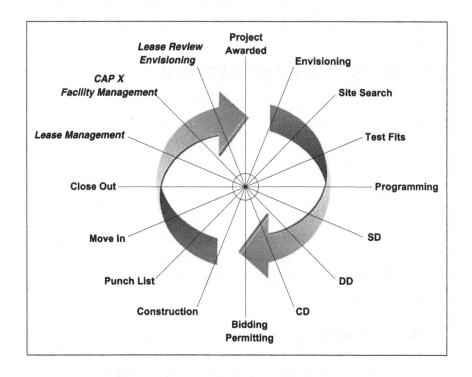

Larger clients need architects and interior designers who are able to provide services to plan and implement daily moves, adds, and changes; perform space analysis; calculate departmental chargebacks; and perform restacking services. Those firms with the desire, capability, and recognition of the importance of Day 2 services do very well.

Fast Forward to 2018:

Link Systems has been widely successful. Over the years, more than 500 companies have used its facility management system, and over 700 of the largest corporations use ProLease to manage their leased and owned properties. We have added WorkOrder/Preventative Maintenance and Equipment Leasing modules to make ProLease one of the most robust integrated real estate applications. In addition, we have continued with our portfolio manager product for building owners to track and report on millions of square feet of tenant-leased spaces.

Architects must start thinking 360 if they want to expand their services and remain competitive. As I mentioned, "nonliability" services are being copied from other professionals. The AIA and IFMA need to take aggressive measures to change the focus of the young members in the profession.

VENDOR VS. STRATEGIC PARTNER

This section may be the most important of all the tips and suggestions included in the book. Unless you have been the client, it is hard for you as the architect to understand how important and how easy it is to be a strategic partner.
Let us first look at the definitions of each.

Vendor—A vendor is anyone who provides goods or services to a company or individuals. Most architectural and design firms, engineers, contractors, furniture dealers, etc., fall into this category. While they do a great job of providing professional services according to the contract, on time and on budget, they are missing huge opportunities for additional services.

Strategic Partner—A strategic partner is a vendor on steroids, one who knows when and how to perform above and beyond contract deliverables by delivering additional project metrics to help the corporate facility manager deal positively with internal management. A strategic partner learns how to repackage information used on the main project so that it becomes valuable for future use.

When architects understand that they need to deliver a much different service to be considered a strategic partner, only then will fees not be calculated as a commodity, but rather from a value basis, as other professionals' fees are.

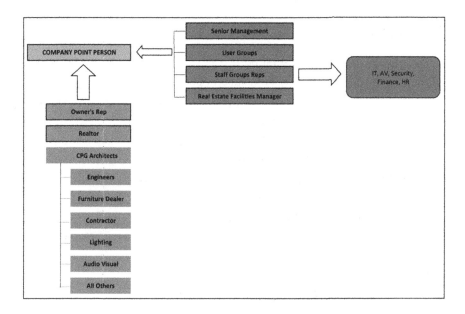

Most of the architects I know treat projects on a "one-off" basis, and management stresses to the staff to keep to the requirements in the contract. When staff veers off from a set series of tasks and starts doing work not in the contract, even when asked by the client, the time spent may not be reimbursable, and the time lost may be critical to meeting the schedule.

Everybody has a boss. The company's point person whom you deal with is certainly no exception and most likely has a number of people giving direction and firing questions at him or her both throughout the project and after the project is complete. In the process of preparing services on any project, there is a tremendous amount of information gathered by the architect that should be repackaged and given back to the client's point person, so they can answer management's follow-up questions in a timely basis. The following list includes some of the questions I was asked on a daily basis in my role as Director of

Planning and Design at American Express. Having information readily available was crucial to being successful and well respected.

Architects need to ask their client contacts what kinds of questions they will be asked so they can deliver the data. Here are some of the questions I needed to be prepared to answer on any given day:

Frequently Asked Questions of Corporate Real Estate and Facilities Managers

Lease questions

- When is/are our lease(s) up?
- Do we have an early termination option?
- Do we have an option to expand?
- Do we have a renewal option?
- What is our remaining lease obligation?
- Do we have the right to sublet?
- What critical leases are coming due next year?
- What are the lease notification dates?
- What are staff personnel/space projections next year?
- Do we have to lease more space next year to accommodate growth?

Buy/build questions

- How long did it take to construct the building?
- What were our site/acquisition costs per gross square foot?
- What were our core and shell costs per gross square foot?
- What were the interior fit-up costs per usable square foot? Furniture fixtures and finishes/usable square foot?
- What were the costs for all consultants as a percentage of total costs?
- What were the costs per trade on a GSF basis?

Space questions

- Can we subdivide to sublet the surplus space?
- What will the cost be to subdivide?

- What is our utilization of space per building?
- What are our loss factors per building—usable square feet (USF) to rentable square feet (RSF)?
- We need to find space for (25) people—what are our options?
- How much space does each group occupy—what are the chargebacks?

Schedule questions

- When do we need to get the staff groups involved to start the project?
- When do we need the architect on board?
- Are we on schedule to move in as planned? What will not be finished?
- When will everything be finished? When do you want our seating chart?
- What is our employee move plan?

Cost questions

- What did it cost us to renovate? USF/RSF/GSF
- What were all our total costs for this project? USF/RSF/GSF
- Did we stay within our AR (Appropriation Request)?
- What is the breakdown of costs by trade?
- What percentage is the furniture cost of the total per USF/RSF?

THE VALUE OF BEING A STRATEGIC PARTNER

You know you have received partner status when you have learned something of fundamental importance to your client's business and are regarded as "one of us." You know you are stuck in a vendor-like world when no one seems to listen to your ideas and your client thinks of you as replaceable. So, make yourself valuable, and you will be rewarded. Following are some clear perks to becoming a strategic partner:

Partners receive timely payments.

Vendors sometimes have to wait for payment well after the work is done, are held to a strict schedule, and may be penalized for missing deadlines.

Partners engage with clients in a spirit of cooperation and open communications.
Vendors are told what the client wants them to hear and when they want them to hear it.

Partners build trust with clients and commit to making the relationship a win-win situation.
Vendors are kept on a short leash and are often pushed to perform beyond the scope of work without additional compensation.

Partners focus on delivering on an ongoing basis measurable results that are aligned to business objectives and values.
Vendors are accountable to billable hours related to tasks that are often not connected to strategic business goals.

Partners are asked to help set the agenda.
Vendors are told what the client wants done.

Partners earn business based on demonstrated expertise, business value, and cultural fit.
Vendors secure the work by slashing their price, being willing to make concessions, and hoping something more profitable is in the cards for them in the future.

Partners are human: they make and admit their mistakes, for which they are forgiven.
Vendors must watch their actions very closely and are more likely to be in trouble when they make mistakes.

Partners are viewed as advisers and have their client's ear.
Vendors are looked upon as a potential adversary who, if not managed properly, could cause trouble and would then get fired.

The relationship you *want* to have with a client is as a strategic partner, not a vendor.

Here is one way to deliver valuable information back to your contact after the project is complete. Giving back valuable information is the difference between being a good vendor or service provider and being a strategic partner.

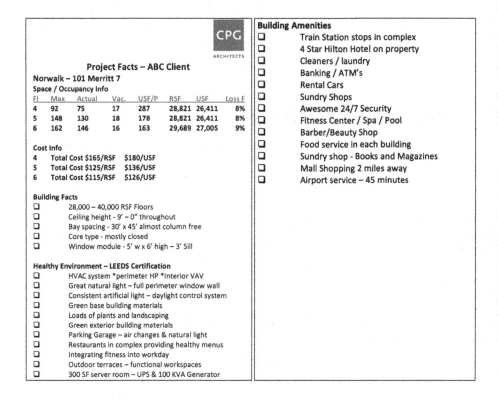

CPG
ARCHITECTS

Project Facts – ABC Client

Norwalk – 101 Merritt 7

Space / Occupancy Info

Fl	Max	Actual	Vac.	USF/P	RSF	USF	Loss F
4	92	75	17	287	28,821	26,411	8%
5	148	130	18	178	28,821	26,411	8%
6	162	146	16	163	29,689	27,005	9%

Cost Info

4	Total Cost $165/RSF	$180/USF
5	Total Cost $125/RSF	$136/USF
6	Total Cost $115/RSF	$126/USF

Building Facts
- 28,000 – 40,000 RSF Floors
- Ceiling height - 9' – 0" throughout
- Bay spacing - 30' x 45' almost column free
- Core type - mostly closed
- Window module - 5' w x 6' high – 3' Sill

Healthy Environment – LEEDS Certification
- HVAC system *perimeter HP *Interior VAV
- Great natural light – full perimeter window wall
- Consistent artificial light – daylight control system
- Green base building materials
- Loads of plants and landscaping
- Green exterior building materials
- Parking Garage – air changes & natural light
- Restaurants in complex providing healthy menus
- Integrating fitness into workday
- Outdoor terraces – functional workspaces
- 300 SF server room – UPS & 100 KVA Generator

Building Amenities
- Train Station stops in complex
- 4 Star Hilton Hotel on property
- Cleaners / laundry
- Banking / ATM's
- Rental Cars
- Sundry Shops
- Awesome 24/7 Security
- Fitness Center / Spa / Pool
- Barber/Beauty Shop
- Food service in each building
- Sundry shop - Books and Magazines
- Mall Shopping 2 miles away
- Airport service – 45 minutes

CAP X BUDGET PLANNING: WHAT IS IT?

Capital expenditure planning (CAP X) includes the people and procedures a business relies on to evaluate *long-term needs* and assess *long-term business requirements*. Comparing needs to long-term plans and business growth objectives helps the business prioritize and plan for capital asset purchases. In some cases, this can be as simple as inspecting the roof, assessing its remaining useful life and the cost of replacement, and then adding to a capital expenditure plan in order of priority.

In other cases, however, capital expenditure planning can be significantly more complicated. For example, upgrading an IT infrastructure typically must be planned in a series of stages that can span a period of months or years.

What projects are necessary for next year and what are the estimated budgets and schedules listed by infrastructure costs vs. renovation costs vs. new building costs? What projects would it be nice to do next year, and what are the estimated budgets and schedules listed by infrastructure costs vs. renovation costs vs. new building costs?

Architects, sometimes in conjunction with others, should provide this service to corporations. Think of the service as a punch list for future work. Done well, the service adds to the architect's backlog that is often performed without bidding on an hourly basis—not fixed fee.

MANAGING CASH FLOW

Everything I read about businesses that fail suggests that they did not have adequate funds to start or they did not manage cash flow well. Unless there are some real problems with the product or service, the management of income is critical to having a healthy business.

 After I was in business for a year or so, I asked our accountant how I could better handle and hopefully reduce our expenses. I was trying to figure out how much we should spend in each of the expense categories on the balance sheet. The answer I got surprised me. He said, "Spend 99 percent of your time working on projects and getting new business," let qualified people manage the expenses, and you will be fine. *Do not micromanage the expenses.*

I was fortunate to have a qualified person, my wife, managing the money, so I did what our accountant suggested and have never looked back. I must be one of the only owners in the country who has never signed a check. We also have a superb CFO who has managed the office and finances for about 25 years. My wife quit after 10 years to start an art appreciation program for an international auction house. She started our company with expert direction, and I continued the winning approach by hiring the best person I could find to do the day-to-day finances. That way I could focus on making connections and growing the business.

 Most architects I know complain constantly about the amount of office management they need to do. *I do none.* I check into things now and again, but generally I leave those job functions to others.

The other advice our first accountant gave us was to get our billing out as close to the first of each month as we could. This takes a lot more organization than you think, to get the time sheets in, collate project reimbursable expenses, and include subcontractors' invoices. It also takes some fancy technology, which we developed to do this. A manual system would never work for us. The first day of each month, our senior staff reviews draft invoices and makes any updates or modifications that are necessary. Then, a button is pushed and the invoices print, along with the related reimbursable pages.

We credit this effort in getting invoices paid promptly.

Here is how our firm's expenses break down, in terms of costs we consider fixed (nondiscretionary—79 percent) and those we have some control over (discretionary costs—21 percent):

Nondiscretionary

Salaries	Equipment lease
Rent	Legal/accounting/recruitment
Business insurance	Interest
Business taxes	Repairs/maintenance
Telephone	Depreciation
Freight/postage	401K expense
Office supplies	Professional license fees

Discretionary

Bonuses	Training
Client contract labor	Profit sharing
Company car	Donations
Public relations and advertising	Credit card merchant expense
Travel	Dues
Meals and entertainment	Subcontractors/internet/software maintenance

Focus on marketing and getting new or repeat business, and let a qualified person manage day-to-day expenses.

MANAGING RISK

Risk is a very broad subject that requires much more attention than a paragraph in this book. The definitive book on the subject of risk in the architectural profession is *Managing Project Risk* by James Atkins and Grant Simpson, and I highly recommend it.

First, let's separate client risk and consultant risk. If the consulting architect does not present their case thoroughly as to the services they propose and the way they intend to run the project, the client may feel it is too risky to se-lect that firm. To put it very simply, if the client believes there will be too much risk hiring you, then you will not have to worry about your own risk. There are three different types of clients, and each has its own issues to be aware of. The client could be:

- The owner of the company who chooses to run the project him/herself
- A staff person assigned to run the project
- An owner's rep or project manager

Each of these situations has different levels of risk for the consulting team. Risk is something the consultants need to discuss as they determine their fee and prepare for the presentation. This subject of risk should be an important part of the presentation.

Client Risks

- The project will come in over budget
- The project will not be completed within the approved schedule
- The project will not look like it should
- The project will have design flaws—things may not fit
- The design may not have anticipated space for needed equipment
- Selected materials do not perform or wear as planned
- Parts of the design do not meet code
- Engineering flaws such as mechanical systems were not properly sized for the load, or equipment is too noisy

There are many things the client may not like; some are minor and some can escalate, depending on who initiates the concern. The owner's rep really has two bosses—the company person assigned to the project, and the manage-ment team. The company person assigned to the project may have only one higher level to be concerned about. Prior to the interview process, it is hard to find out if the client has a history for being litigious, but it makes sense to try and find out.

Consulting Team Risks

Your risks are usually the same as the client's, but from a different perspective.

Here is my approach to avoiding risks:

1. When the consulting team is being assembled, share the contract you have with the client with the others: MEP, lighting, acoustical, AV, IT, CM, etc., and have them agree to the terms in your contract. When they prepare their own contracts, through you or directly with the client, they should reference all the same terms and conditions as yours.
2. When the consulting team is signed up, all should meet to discuss the scope of work each believes they agreed to do to make sure nothing has fallen through the cracks. The consulting team should verbally walk through the project to discuss scope, timing, potential costs, and potential areas of risk.
3. The architect should meet with the client or their representative to have the same discussion.

If the architect does just these few steps, it should help the team avoid the majority of unnecessary claims.

First, when budgets are prepared, each consulting group should approve and be responsible for its own budget.

Second, if bids come in higher than the approved budget, after alternates are taken into account, the bids need to be compared to original estimates, and each trade(s) or consultant(s) is responsible to work with the client to make changes to get back within the approved budget.

If the client decides to make reductions in a trade/consultant's work that was within budget, that group should be reimbursed for its time.

If an issue comes up that you believe will be serious, take time to investigate it, then deal with the issue head-on with the client. If the issue has to do with one of the other consultants, get them involved immediately. If appropriate, let your insurer know of the problem as early as you can.

Most situations work themselves out by being honest, sincere, and available to the client.

USING TECHNOLOGY

Technology and IT professionals are expensive and must be used wisely. As you have a business plan for your architectural business, you should have a business plan for your IT needs, as well. After staff salaries, your IT-related costs might be your second greatest expense, followed by rent or real estate ownership—especially if you include the cost of your technology team and related software and hardware costs. This surprises most firms because they think real estate occupancy costs are second greatest after salaries.

Technology costs creep up on you during the year. There are a number of software and cloud costs that are now subscription based, and you don't get a real monthly bill—they are automatically deducted from your credit card. Depending on the size of your firm, AutoCAD/Revit upgrades can be expensive, and training for that software is expensive when you figure in the loss of billable hours during training.

Technology staffs are now permitting individuals to use their own equipment in conjunction with the office-provided workstations and software. For many companies, this means the introduction and integration with Apple products; iPhones, iPads and iBooks are now as common as the desktop AutoCAD station.

As staff start to use personal software applications on the network, all of this needs to be integrated, protected, and backed up with all the firm's other applications.

The ease with which one can download software apps from the Apple app store is both good and bad. It is good in that staff can now, for very little cost, try new applications that may help them in their work; and bad in the sense that as these apps are used on the networks, there are unforeseen consequences. Today the IT professional has his/her hands full as new types of software become even easier to retrieve.

Even small offices have lots of software to deal with. For example:

- 3D Max
- Adobe Acrobat Standard XI
- Adobe Illustrator
- Adobe Photoshop
- Aperture
- AutoCAD
- AutoCAD Architecture
- Equitrac Office
- FileMaker Pro 14
- FileZilla for FTP
- Firefox
- Google Chrome
- I Render NXT for Sketch up
- Internet Explorer
- Jungle Disk
- Mac Keynote
- Mac Numbers
- Mac Word
- Microsoft Access 2013
- Microsoft Excel

- Microsoft OneNote
- Microsoft PowerPoint
- Microsoft Project 2013
- Microsoft Word
- Parallels for Mac
- QuarkXPress
- Revit

- Roxio
- ShoreTel Communicator
- SketchUp Pro 2015
- Solid Capture
- Symantec Endpoint Protection
- WinZip

HOW GOOD IS YOUR WORKFLOW PROCESS?

I think most businesses believe they have well-defined processes and procedures in place. Sometimes we are just too close to the situation to realize that a few tweaks could make a significant change in timing and profitability. The problem is that either we don't want to take the time or we don't want to admit there might be a better way.

Like most, at our firm we thought our steps were well defined until I talked at lunch one day with a friend who is in the millwork business. He was frustrated that as his business grew, the company continued to add staff. Finding qualified manufacturing staff is very difficult, especially in states like Connecticut with high labor rates. They knew they had real inefficiencies and needed to change but were too busy to stop and review their process.

Hearing the story of how they found and hired a consulting group called CONNSTEP was inspiring. CONNSTEP helped them objectively analyze their workflow. With many small tweaks, they were able to dramatically change their paperwork process and shop procedures to be able to effectively take on additional business *without adding staff*.

I realized architects are also in the manufacturing business; we manufacture a set of plans so that buildings and interiors can be built. Like our millwork friends, we were not looking to be more efficient to *reduce* our staff, we were looking to be more efficient to be able to take on *additional work with the same staff*.

Our experience working with CONNSTEP was great. We put together a team to identify all the steps in our process and identified those steps that led to churn. By working more diligently to get key information much earlier in the planning process, we are able to reduce or eliminate the churn that eats up time and profits.

We found churn was killing us in every step in the process.

- We were starting projects before we had a real understanding of clients' goals.
- We prepared test fits for buildings without complete program information from the client.
- We were starting conceptual plans without all the consultants on board.
- Without the consultants on board, we could not deliver a complete budget.

In summary, our steps and processes were driven by others.

To solve the problem, we changed our process, changed the sequence of our deliverables to our client, and changed their expectation of timing. We are now able to move faster and much more accurately.

IMPORTANCE OF INTERNAL SHARING

I find that, while we think it is human nature to want to share ideas and information, that does not happen automatically in business unless your company has a specific application for office management, including:

- Contact Management
- Contracts
- Potential/Awarded projects
- Time tracking and billing
- Project reporting

Employees tend to do things the way they want and let it be others' responsibility for coordinating and aggregating the numbers. With the myriad programs and apps available to the firm, it is very easy to coordinate all the data generated every day.

Another aspect of sharing, we could call it external sharing, is how you treat client project deliverables, and who is copied or who has access to specific information. The client sends very little to the architect during the course of the project in terms of specific schedule, budget, staffing/space, or product specifications and counts on the architect to collate and disseminate all this information for them.

When the architect treats each document it sends out as an individual document, it is much more difficult for the client to understand and process the information. It makes it much more difficult for the client to reply to questions in a timely fashion. On the other hand, if the architect treats all deliverables within a coordinated package, the client has a much easier time understanding the big picture and the implications of their approvals and decisions.

SETTING UP THE OFFICE TO SCALE

When you start out on your own, it is hard to know what the future holds. You may know the direction you want to take, the type of work you want to do, and the size of the firm you can handle individually or with partners.

What I have frequently seen happen is that a firm starts down one path and meets an important client who gives them a few plum assignments, spurring their growth in an unexpected direction. Or a firm that does corporate and retail work gets a chance to do an educational project that receives recognition, and they continue to do work as educational architects.

It is very hard to scale for this. We did three things:

1. We made sure our internal processes were as automated as possible and the technology could handle a lot more volume. Storage capacity is very cheap, and cloud solutions enable staff to work from any location.
2. We made sure we had tremendous flexibility in our office location so growth could be handled without a major move. We have expanded four times within the same building.
3. We made sure we looked at adding multitalented staff.

INTERVIEWING

Finding our second employee was easy. As noted before, I had a very smart wife who reluctantly came on board to help me get started. There was no interview process, no résumé to review, no salary negotiations, and no discussion of benefits. Hiring the next few employees was much more difficult. You really need to find the most well-rounded architects you can find, since you cannot be everywhere. Having staff who can stand in for you is critical. While the pool of talent in our area was small, and still is, we were fortunate to find a few good folks. Two of the originals are still with us over 30 years later.

Over the years, interviewers develop styles, and mine is very casual. I preferred to just chat rather than ask specific questions. That way I can weave in my questions at the appropriate time. This approach makes the interview much longer, but I know I got a better feel for the individual. I like to know where and how they grew up and whether they had sisters and brothers. I should add that I try not to look at the résumé before the interview and let the flow of the conversation walk them through their experiences—both good and bad.

Most people are ready for the typical questions, like what your best experiences were and what you think you do best. I like to ask what they think they are bad at, where they will need help, and what they want to learn that will help them be a better architect or designer. I try to find out if they have desires to someday start their own firm and, if so, how they plan to accomplish it.

In the early years, I tried to have interviews at my house so the process could be more relaxed and not have normal office disturbances. Second best is in a quiet restaurant; the worst place for the first interview is in the office. I do not think many interviewers understand that applicants are also interviewing the firm to see if they like the business, quality of work, and staff members, and finally whether the salary and benefits meet their needs. By interviewing out of the office, I can determine if there might be a good fit for us both and, if so, invite them back for a second interview in the office so they can ask their questions, meet the staff, and find out if they like us.

Those two steps certainly take longer, but our chance of hiring employees who know what they are getting into is much greater. How many times have you heard a new employee say, "I didn't know I would be working on that project or for that person" or, "Wow, the benefits really aren't very good"?

I find it harder to interview today because there is so much more to talk about. When we started, there were no discussions about CAD, since it was all by hand; no discussions about software and technology, since there was none; no need to understand rendering techniques, because everything was drawn by hand. For years, we never had to discuss time management because there were few distractions during the office day. No one had cell phones, Facebook pages, or personal email addresses. Everyone had just an office phone, so if you got or placed a call, everyone else knew it and could often hear your conversation.

It is always preferable in the second interview to have a few people interview the applicant so you can compare different points of view. I try for one of the interviewers to be the person the applicant will report to. Also, having them meet other employees often makes them more relaxed when asked questions. Hiring a new person is expensive, if you add the time to interview and the time to train them to get up to speed to be productive and billable.

It seems more customary today for professional applicants to take some kind of a test than it was years ago. Staff assistant applicants often take typing or composition tests, so why not design applicants? We ask some beginning designers to take a simple planning test to see if they can do basic tasks as they presented in their portfolio. We sometimes ask more senior designers to do a small few-hour design project.

The reason I do not place a lot of importance on the résumé is that much of it is too vague or may even be inaccurate. You never really know what someone did on a project listed on his or her résumé. I find it more beneficial to try to find out how they think and will react in certain situations.

Younger applicants, those with just a couple of years of experience, can really surprise you by having many additional qualities that could benefit the firm. Those in their twenties have grown up with unbelievable technology and are often quite knowledgeable about social media, website construction, software applications, and new ways of marketing products and services. These talents should not be overlooked by older interviewers.

When it is time to discuss salary and benefits, I recommend talking about the two at the same time, perhaps even starting with the benefits package. If your benefits package is competitive, hearing about it before the salary figures may make a positive difference to the applicant. Then you can approach salary discussions by either stating what the position pays or asking first what they are looking for. Negotiation is a good thing.

ETHICS

Treat clients and other professionals well, and you will do just fine. However, if you do something that causes someone not to trust you, that news spreads like wildfire. As stated in a previous section, "What goes around comes around" is a topic we discuss with all new hires. If you think each new person was taught how to act from their previous employer, you may be mistaken. What you will tell them will probably not be repetitive, and if it is, it is another reminder about the way they should conduct their business. We all know of the saying "We have one chance to make a good first impression." Similarly, once your reputation is tarnished, that is how people might see you for a long time. It is hard to recover from a bad reputation, especially when you work in a smaller setting. Management must set a professional example for the staff to follow.

Our firm used to have a clause in our proposal saying, "The only fees we receive are from our client and others may, to have a more competitive fee, accept spec fees from manufacturers or vendors." We ask that all firms competing on the project sign this clause to make sure we are all evaluated on a level playing field.

After one of our larger potential clients said they didn't care who was on the "take" as long as they got the lowest costs, we were so disillusioned, we stopped making a point of including that clause in our contract.

We were not selected for that project, and the firm selected was fired before it was completed. Being honest and direct usually wins out in the end.

RESPONSIBILITIES TO STAFF

Owners have many responsibilities to staff. After many years, staff is like family and should be treated as such. CPG has four employees who have been with us for over 30 years, many for 20 to 25 years, and many for over 10 years. The firm must either pay too much or let them have too much fun and freedom, or they like the challenging and creative atmosphere.

The firm also has the responsibility to act in a professional way. If someone is sick, the firm sticks with them; if they are in some kind of trouble, the firm helps them find help; if someone is getting ready to take the exam, the firm pays for their courses and materials.

We try to have competitive benefits, but also personal benefits that help families. All families and firms are challenged with healthcare issues and are troubled with rising costs, and we wish we could do more.

THE WORK ENVIRONMENT

Many architects' offices seem sterile, and I am not sure why. Architects' projects are anything but sterile. I personally go overboard the other way and like the office to include all the toys, games, and gadgets I like to play with. We display antiques and have a rotation of items like these:

- Slot machines
- Juke box
- Fortune-telling machines
- Circus wheels
- Circus softball toss

- Pool table
- Pinball
- Test Your Grip
- Gumball and nut machines

Clients love the look and are encouraged to play the games. It certainly breaks the ice with prospective and new clients.

I encourage everyone to express his or her own personality in their work area. We occupy space in an old mill building that has brick walls, wood ceilings 12' high, wood columns, exposed mechanicals, and large windows. The environment is exciting every day—even after 31 years of being there.

My recommendation is to get the most exciting space you can find—I have always said to our clients that space is an asset. Great space helps you attract talent, and clients love to come there for meetings. Our rental costs are 4 percent of expenses, so splurge on the best space.

WORKING WITH FAMILY

It was not too long after we started the firm that my wife had some frustrations about how we were going to work together. My wife asked me, "Do you want to be right all the time or do you want to be happy?" I did not give it a second thought—I said, "I want to be happy." To this day, 35 years later, I am often not right, but I am a very happy guy.

After my son graduated from Tulane in 1995, he announced he would like to spend some time skiing in Colorado, taking after my wife and her love for the sport. My answer was that is fine; you just have to earn the money to get out there and pay for your living expenses. He asked if he could work for our real estate software company, Link Systems, to save enough to make the trip. That was 20 years ago, and he never left. Now he owns the company. Working with family can be great.

We have had many staff members who have brought their kids to work on special projects. One of our staff member's nephews, an architect, worked for us for a number of years and was tremendous. Now his niece has been with us for a few years, and she is cut from the same fabulous cloth.

Having staff members' kids work in the afternoons, on holidays, or in the summer is a real plus—good for the parents, and good for the kids to understand how business works.

IS IT POSSIBLE TO HAVE A PERFECT CLIENT?

Yes—it does happen every once and a while, and when it does, the firm talks about the project for years after it is complete. A perfect project is one where all the stars align and every minute is pure bliss. We have had just one perfect project in our 35-year history. It was Diageo's US Headquarters, a 100,000-RSF relocation from eight existing locations. Diageo is one of the world's largest producers of adult beverages, producing spirits, beer, and wine.

We hope all architects and clients learn from Diageo's approach. Here is why this project was special:

- The VP of Real Estate, Ki Gaillard, was very experienced and knew what she was looking for in an architect. Ki was truly an imaginative thinker and manager, enabling the project to be successful for all.
- The RFP process was extremely well organized. Those who were invited to participate got together and listened to the company's vision from a cost, schedule, branding, and employee point of view. Ki talked about their current facilities and what they wanted to do differently. She talked about Diageo's clients and the image they wanted to project. She talked about staffing growth, standards, and all the needs for all special areas. Ki covered everything expected in an RFP, and all the architects heard it firsthand at the same time.
- Questions were permitted, and I noticed how the mood changed from one where competitors were on edge with one another to an environment where competitors participated and talked about ways to make the project better.
- The process for selecting the firm was based on a design competition for which Diageo *compensated* each firm that participated. Firms were given three weeks to prepare their presentations, which was plenty of time.
- There were *no restrictions* regarding presentation techniques— we chose to do large boards with all freehand concept sketches. We also decided to document the process we went through in developing our ideas over the three weeks and presented each week in the form of an eight-page playbill. This showed Diageo how the entire office pitched in to produce the presentation.
- When it became time for us to present, we served sherbet in iced cups, so the client could "refresh their palate" after the prior presentation. We dressed alike and wore nametags with titles so they remembered us.
- Each participant was given two hours to make their presentation—*no one was rushed* and there was plenty of time for discussion at the end, so the Diageo team understood the concepts and reasons for the ideas.
- Following our presentation, we got a call saying that Ki would like to come to our office and meet with the team. *Telling us*

in person that we got the job was unbelievable. It had never happened that a client came to our office to say they wanted to work with us, and I cannot tell you how wonderful she made us feel. She also brought champagne for the entire firm. You know the saying, *"If something starts right, there is a better chance for it to end right."*

Finding the Perfect Home

The first step in the process was the preparation of personnel and space projections, including departmental growth requirements that were used to evaluate potential buildings. Eight buildings were evaluated, and the winner was a nine-story building that had just begun construction. There were two problems that we thought might be deal breakers: first, the building was larger than needed, and second, the core layout was not efficient for the client's use. The developer and his architect agreed to our changes—we proposed eliminating one floor, redesigned all the cores, and changed the configuration of the terrace on the new upper floor to accommodate outdoor dining for the employee cafeteria, bar, and conference center.

Research

We did a lot of research visiting bars around the country; the bar in the head-quarters was a key design element, as well as corporate dining rooms, conference centers, and fitness facilities.

New ways of working

Diageo was ahead of the curve in deciding that their new workplace would be collaborative, flexible, and efficient. There would be 1,000 employees, and the company decided there were to be no offices—even for the CEO and management team. They specified only one station size. VPs and up occupied two stations. We designed furniture mock-ups and each manufacturer selected to present was compensated for their solution. Steelcase provided the best solution and was awarded the furniture contract.

Enclaves

Enclaves, small two-person meeting areas, were spread around the floors, and each floor had a number of various-sized, product-branded conference rooms.

Collaboration

The main pantry on each floor was horseshoe-shaped, located right off the elevator bank, so employees coming to the floor could see friends and chat. All the banquettes at the perimeter of the café had Wi-Fi, for small group meetings.

Branding

Every hallway, conference room, and elevator cab was tastefully branded with product groupings based on the groups occupying the floor. Clients and employees loved it.

Projects like this do not happen by accident. You need a company that really cares about its staff and has a dynamic leader with the experience to creatively push the consultants and enough time to explore the options.

Ki Gaillard was the best client we have ever had. She hit every button perfectly, from the creative way she invited firms to bid on the project, to the well-designed RFP and contract, to permitting time for research. We are grateful for Ki's efforts.

Even the elevators were branded by product line.

PART VI

Time, Money, and Luck

CHAPTER 13

Numbers Matter

Now do not laugh. Many people I have met go into business just because they think it will be fun and exciting. While they hope they will make some money, they find out very quickly that "HOPE" is not a good plan and end up being a statistic. The statistics I read about most frequently are that 75 percent of new design firms fail in the first three years, and only 30 percent of the remaining makes it to 10 years. Only about 8 percent make it past the 10-year mark.

When you explore how most firms start, it is easy to understand why the number of survivors is so low. However, if you plan well and stay focused, success is almost guaranteed.

Most firms start with one or more architects leaving a firm and taking a project or two from their current employer. This may seem like a safe way to begin your journey, but only if the project is large enough and has enough billing remaining to keep the doors open. You need this so you can establish a presence in the marketplace and start looking for your next projects. Of course, your employer may not be so quick to let you make off with a client. It is challenging to multitask: working on a project, developing a business plan, setting up a website, and perhaps having to hire a full-time or part-time employee or two to do the work while you do the marketing and all the other things discussed in previous chapters. Do not forget about having your accountant set up the books, timesheets, and billing system. Other not-so-minor tasks are selecting and continually upgrading IT equipment, telephone systems, and mobile services.

Others start firms when a major client gives or promises work when they start a firm. This approach also sounds great on the surface. Murphy's Law suggests it might be too good to be true, and it is understood that a million things can go wrong. The project may not start, but if it does, it may not be funded, or like many projects, it may start and stop. I would ask for a written commitment with some kind of a financial guarantee for at least six months—sufficient to keep the doors open while you set up and start marketing.

While the first two methods often work, the best way to start a firm is to have a big trust fund with unlimited dollars. Money in the bank gives a comfort level to start properly with sufficient time to develop a business plan, marketing materials, and website, as well as to staff up with critical positions filled and ready for the work to come in. People always ask me how much they need to start their business, and my answer is always the same: you should have at least enough cash in the bank to carry the planned expenses for six months. When you start a new project, try your best to get a deposit or an advance. As is often said, it is better to work with someone else's money than your own.

I launched the business with no money, no preparation, two little kids at home, and no clients or potential clients. I was not even smart enough to know to be scared. I developed a business plan over the weekend and on Monday morning started calling a few friends to get advice.

All I knew was that failure was not an option and I had to just plow ahead, listening to all the advice I could get from people I trusted. Thirty-six years later, I could not be more pleased with all the staff that worked with us, the consultants we co-operated with, and the clients we served. It has been extremely challenging and rewarding. Here are a couple of things to keep in mind as you get started:

- Staffing of the three skills needed initially, marketing, design, and finance—How many of these skills will be handled by the principal(s) starting the business?
- Business—Do you have a project to start or do you have one that will "definitely" start when you hang out your shingle? If so, will the potential income carry the firm's overhead for a number of months?
- Finance and office management—Have you set up your technology, website, financial systems, payroll, etc.?

LEARNING FROM OTHERS

There are many people we can learn from, but there is a special group of related professionals who have always inspired me in the way they start and run their businesses. These professionals drive trucks or vans and provide both commercial and residential services. They have the same issues in starting their businesses: marketing, writing proposals, scheduling the work, managing staff, sending invoices, and collecting quickly to manage cash flow.

They start their business in a similar fashion to architects, usually by leaving a company where they have apprenticed. They may take an account or two to start and then find themselves in a similar marketing mode to look for the next client. We all find it is difficult to properly service a client and look for new business at the same time. These entrepreneurs are the plumbers, electricians, HVAC contractors, drywall contractors, and flooring installers. Similar to architects, most have had very little business training. What impresses me is that their strategy is mostly intuitive and their desire is not to change the world. Their ambitions are grounded and realistic. They are focused on keeping the work and paychecks coming, keeping clients happy, and keeping their gas tanks full. Their networks for sharing leads are often effective without the overhead burden of endless emails, tweets, and instant messages.

They start their businesses to have a better life for themselves and their families. What impresses me is the way the trades work together, cover for one another, and share potential project information.

Perhaps architects should drive vans with their company names stenciled on the side, with AIA registration numbers and liability insurance numbers in bold type. It is interesting to compare these contractors' business statistics with architectural firms:

Profession	# of Businesses	# of Employees
Plumbers	115,737	468,869
Electricians	214,000	968,000
HVAC Contractors	104,288	468,773
Architectural Firms	20,836	146,277

After all my years in the business, I am constantly surprised at how few architectural firms there are in the country.

INITIAL STAFFING

The three most important functions in any architectural or interior design firm are:

1. **Marketing**—The person or team who has responsibility to identify and bring in the business. A supply of new business is necessary for all organizations. We do not use the title Marketing Director, Marketing PIC, or any title with the words "business development" in it. That expression is often negative to the client. In smaller firms, clients expect to work with a principal who will be managing and leading the project. Clients know the marketing folks are in only until the sale is made, and then on to another opportunity, never to be seen again. The marketing position needs to be filled by a principal or certainly a senior person. I have seen many firms hire "marketing specialists" that are door openers who get paid a commission for new work, and then when they leave, all the leads and contact information go with them to their next marketing job.
2. **Design**—There must be a person in charge of design. This creative position has responsibility for a number of related functions, as shown on the following chart.
3. **Finances**—This person wears many hats and definitely needs to be a multitasker. When an office is small, this person may be able to function by himself or herself. As the office grows, additional staff will be required to fulfill functions such as Receptionist, Office Manager, Accountant, Administrative Assistant, Marketing Team, Social Media Manager, IT Director, etc.

All three positions are *critical* to the development of the office.

A three-legged stool is the perfect analogy. Without perfect balance to manage workflow, design/production, and accounting, the firm may become a bit shaky. When work comes in too fast, design and production may suffer; when work comes in slowly, staff tends to panic and worry about their jobs. If invoices are not sent out promptly and accurately at the beginning of each month, bills cannot be paid in a timely fashion. While the individuals in charge of the three functional areas many not be equal partners or even owners, the responsibility of the functions is certainly equal.

When a business starts, it may not be financially possible for all three positions to be filled. A founder may try to do two or even all three of the functions themselves depending on their capabilities. I always advise founders to try to fill all the positions as soon as possible.

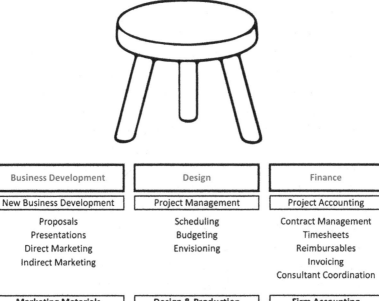

Business Development	Design	Finance
New Business Development	**Project Management**	**Project Accounting**
Proposals	Scheduling	Contract Management
Presentations	Budgeting	Timesheets
Direct Marketing	Envisioning	Reimbursables
Indirect Marketing		Invoicing
		Consultant Coordination
Marketing Materials	**Design & Production**	**Firm Accounting**
Advertising	Test Fits	
Blog	Conceptual Planning	**Human Resources**
Branding	Envisioning	Employee Manual
Photography	FF & E	
Promotion	Documentation	**Office Management**
Social Media	Construction Observation	
Website	Punch list	
	Move Planning	
	Close Out	

FINANCE 101 FOR ARCHITECTS

There are a few things architects need to know about finance:

1. Make sure you have money in the bank.
2. Make sure you do not spend more than you have.
3. Make sure you have some saved for a rainy day.
4. Make sure you have an accountant you trust.

Terminology

There are two main methods of accounting—the cash basis and the accrual basis. Because there are differences in the two approaches, it is recommended that you ask your accountant which method is best for your specific type of business and tax bracket. Carrie Smith provides the following definitions:[4]

What is the cash method?

With the cash basis of accounting, you record income as it is received and expenses as they are paid. This does not take into account any accounts receivable or payables, as it only applies to payments from clients when the cash is in hand and expenses when the transaction clears your bank account.

For example, if you invoice a client for $100,000 on March 1 and receive payment on June 15, you would record the income in June's bookkeeping. This is when the money was received and in hand.

Many small business owners choose the cash method of accounting because it is a simplified bookkeeping process. It is easy to track money as it moves in and out of your bank account because there is no need to record receivables or payables.

Additionally, your small business does not have to pay income tax on revenue until the day it is deposited into your bank account.

One downside to using the cash basis of accounting is that it can produce an inaccurate overall picture of your finances, since it does not account for all incoming revenue or outgoing expenses. It can lead you to believe you're having a very high cash-flow month, when in reality the numbers are a result of last month's work.

What is the accrual method?

The accrual basis of accounting is the complete opposite of the cash method. Income and expenses are recorded when they are billed and earned, regardless of when the money is actually received.

Using the example from above, and applying the accrual basis of accounting, you would record the $100,000 as income in March's bookkeeping, versus in April when you actually received the funds.

The upside to using the accrual method is it gives small business owners a more realistic picture of income and expenses during a cer-

---

4   Carrie Smith, "Cash vs. Accrual Accounting: What's Best for Your Small Business?" *QuickBooks*, accessed March 5, 2018. Available here: https://quickbooks.intuit.com/r/bookkeeping/cash-vs-accrual-accounting-whats-best-small-business/

tain period. This can provide you (and your accountant) with a better overall picture of how your business is doing.

One drawback to the accrual method is that it does not account for cash flow or funds that are available in your bank account. If you do not have careful bookkeeping practices, the accrual-based accounting method can be financially devastating for a small business owner, as your books may show a large amount of revenue while your bank account is completely empty.

Basic financial terms

Assets—These are the economic resources a business has, including the products it has in inventory, the office furniture and supplies purchased for use, and any trademarks or copyrights it owns. These assets count toward the value of a business, since they could be sold if the business experienced difficult times.

Liabilities—This includes any debt accrued by a business in the course of starting, growing, and maintaining its operations, including bank loans, credit card debts, and monies owed to vendors and product manufacturers. Liabilities can be divided into two major types: current, which refers to immediate debts (e.g., money owed to suppliers), and long-term debt, which refers to liabilities (e.g., loans and accounts payable).

Expenses—Business expenses are the costs a company incurs each month in order to operate, including rent, utilities, legal costs, employee salaries, contractor pay, and marketing and advertising costs. To remain financially solid, businesses are often encouraged to keep expenses as low as possible.

Cash Flow—Your cash flow is the overall movement of funds through your business each month, including income and expenses. Businesses track general cash flow to determine long-term solvency. A business's cash flow can be determined by comparing its available cash balance at the beginning and end of a specified period.

Bottom Line—This is the total amount a business has earned or lost at the end of the month. The bottom line is the last financial figure on a ledger. The term can also be used in the context of a business's earnings either increasing or decreasing.

Financial Report—A financial report is a comprehensive account of a business's transactions and expenses, created to give a business oversight of its financial matters. A financial report may be prepared for internal use or external sources, such as potential investors.

Financial Statement—Similar to a financial report, a financial statement lists all of a business's financial activities. However, a financial statement is generally a more formal document, often issued by an accountant or lending institution.

Cash Flow Statement—A cash flow statement shows the money that entered and exited a business during a specific period of time. It generally covers four main categories: operating activities, investing activities, financing activities, and supplemental information.

Income Statement—Also known as a "profit and loss statement," an income statement shows the profitability of a business during a period of time. The income statement looks at a business's revenues and expenses through all of its activities.

Balance Sheet—A business's balance sheet gives a snapshot of the company's financial situation at a given moment. This includes the cash it has on hand, the notes payable it has outstanding, and owner(s) equity in the business.

Profit and Loss—To remain financially healthy, a business must have a regular profit that exceeds its losses. Profits and losses are usually itemized on a profit and loss statement, also known as the income statement defined above.

Capital—In business finance terms, the money a business has in its accounts, assets, and investments is known as capital. In business, there are two major types of capital: debt and equity.

Accounts Receivable—Accounts receivable (A/R) is the amount a business is owed by its clients. Usually the client is notified by invoice of the amount owed, and if not paid, the debt is legally enforceable. On a business's balance sheet, accounts receivable is often logged as an asset.

Depreciation—Over time, a business's assets decrease in value due to the time that has passed since it was purchased. For tax purposes, a business can recover the cost of that depreciation through a deduction.

Valuation—When a business seeks funding from investors, those investors want to know the overall worth of that business. This is accomplished through a valuation, which is an estimate of the overall worth of the business.

INDUSTRY METRICS

It is very difficult to get architectural firm metrics from the AIA. Deltek does some good public reporting of the industry. The following Deltek figures were for year 2015. These metrics and percentages are averages of firms across the country.

Operating Profit on Net Revenue—11.8%
Operating profit on net revenue is calculated by dividing pretax, predistribution profit by net revenue (total revenue minus consultants and other direct expenses, both billable and nonbillable), and multiplying by 100.

Utilization Rate—60%
The utilization rate is calculated by dividing the cost of direct labor (labor charged to projects) by the total labor cost of the firm, and multiplying by 100.

Net Labor Multiplier—2.97
The net labor multiplier is calculated by dividing net revenue by direct labor, the cost of labor charged to projects.

Total Payroll Multiplier—1.77
The total payroll multiplier is calculated by multiplying utilization by net labor multiplier, or by dividing net revenue by total labor.

Overhead Rate—160%

The overhead rate is calculated by dividing total overhead (before distributions) by total direct labor expense, and multiplying by 100.

Net Revenue per Employee—$129,689

Net revenue per employee is calculated by dividing annual net revenue by the average total number of employees during the year, including principals.

Employee Turnover—13.7%

Employee turnover is calculated by dividing the number of employees leaving during the year by the average number of employees during the year.

Average Collection Period—75 Days

The average collection period is calculated by dividing accounts receivable by annual total revenue, and multiplying by 365.

TRACKING THE LIFE OF YOUR ARCHITECTURAL DOLLAR

It all starts when you receive an RFP—the decisions you make and the response you submit determine potential project profitability. Each RFP should receive the same consideration and thoughtful review.

- New project evaluation checklist (discussed in Chapter 8)
- Determine services required/Estimate overall time frame
- Select team, estimate time/phase/person
- Calculate hourly rates
- Prepare fee estimate
- Prepare proposal response

CALCULATING EMPLOYEE HOURLY RATES

Gross Annual Salary	$150,000	$125,000	$75,000
17% Covers	$25,500	$21,250	$12,750
Unemployment			
Social Security			
Health Care			
Life Insurance			
Workers Comp			
Profit Sharing - 3.5%	$5,250	$4,375	$2,625
Bonus - 10%	$15,000	$12,500	$7,500
Net Employee Cost Per Year	$104,250	$86,875	$52,125
Gross Hours Worked/Year	2,080	2,080	2,080
Vacation in Hours	120	120	80
Holiday/Sick Leave	15	15	15
Net Hours Worked Per Year	1,945	1,945	1,985
Net Cost Rate/Hour Worked	$54	$45	$26
Ideal Billing Rate @ 2.50	$134	$112	$66
Ideal Billing Rate @ 2.75	$147	$123	$72
Ideal Billing Rate @ 3.00	$161	$134	$79

YOU WON THE BID—TIME TO NEGOTIATE THE CONTRACT

Even though your firm was selected, there are still a number of scope items, not included in most RFPs, left to negotiate that will impact your final fee:

1. Understand and agree to a final scope of work—compare scope discussed to the scope you included in your proposal, and adjust the fee accordingly.
2. Agree to a time schedule—starting point and ending point. Address the issue in writing as to what happens if the project starts later than planned, stops and starts, or the end point is extended beyond the time frame in the RFP.
3. Agree to payment terms—how much time you will allow between client receipt of invoice until payment is made—suggest 30 days.

4. Agree to definitions of a change order—define scope changes impacting square footage, change in terms of quality and details, change in terms of redoing previously approved work, etc.

5. Understand how the client wants to deal with all the other consultants that may be required. If they want the architect to be involved in writing the RFPs for each type of consultant, leveling the bids, scheduling presentation, and sending out reject/award letters, plan on spending considerable additional time. In addition, if your firm will manage consultants' contracts, then you need to determine a markup percentage to do all this plus preparing separate invoices for each, collecting, and distributing their money. Usually managing and coordinating the other consultants' work product is part of the architect's overall responsibility. The contract work just outlined is over and above normal architectural services.

6. Agree to all insurance limits and requirements.

7. Agree to a detailed schedule of when you expect the client to be available for meetings, presentations, and time frames for reviews and approvals.

8. If the client has already or plans to retain the services of an owner's rep or project manager, there are a few additional things to think about both before you submit your proposal and before you finalize the negotiations. If an owner's rep is on board, it is likely they wrote the RFP and it is likely they did not outline their services.

It is important you find out whether you will be responsible for:

- Review and comment on lease or purchase agreements
- Services described in #5
- Preparation and update of project schedule
- Preparation and update of project budget

These are often the prime services provided by the owner's rep, and you certainly do not want to duplicate or take on these services if someone else is doing them. They are very time-consuming.

SETTING UP THE PROJECT IN A MANAGEMENT SYSTEM

Once the project starts, you will want to be ready to document time and billing information, so the first invoice can go out after the first month, if that is appropriate.

There are many systems on the market for architects that will integrate all your functions into one program. We did not find one we liked or could afford at the time, so we built our own in Filemaker. We integrated the major functions of our business. Our system includes sections for:

- **Contact management**—Employees enter all their company, vendor, and project contacts in the system. No more personal Rolodexes.
- **Potential projects**—When a project is identified as "potential," a form is filled out with as much info as we know at the time about the size, type, location, client, who referred us, etc. This way, we can track our progress in an orderly fashion.
- **Awarded projects**—If awarded the project, we just change the status from "potential" to "awarded" and fill in the remaining information including contract amount, fee type, team list, "invoice to" person, reimbursable info, etc. We set up all financials for easy project modeling and tracking.
- **Time tracking**—When employees are assigned to a project, their timesheets are created automatically. Employees fill in their timesheets daily. If time was not entered for a day, a red flag shows up as a reminder. The timesheet system eliminates most of the problems of staff entering time on the wrong project numbers.
- **Reimbursables**—If there are approved reimbursables, those numbers, with backup receipts, are also set up in the system and printed out with the invoices.
- **Billing**—At the end of the month, we push a few buttons and the invoices are prepared for checking by the Project Manager (PM) and Partner in Charge (PIC). Invoices include all reimbursables.

ROLLING UP THE NUMBERS

Having raw financial data is great, but having automatic reporting is what makes the system hum.

Three important reports to start with:

- Balance sheet
- Income statement
- Cash flow statement

Other key reports:

- Tracking actual hours spent per phase against time budgeted per phase
- Tracking value of time spent per phase against dollars budgeted per phase
- Payment history—how quickly our invoices are paid—by client type
- Utilization rate (total billed hours total staff hours available = utilization rate)
- Overhead rate (total overhead costs total direct labor costs = overhead rate)
- Breakeven rate
- Effective multiplier (total revenue direct labor costs = effective multiplier)
- Profit-to-earnings ratio
- Net revenue per employee (total revenue FTE staff = revenue per employee)
- Gross profit margin

Special reports for each project:

- By partner in charge and by lead designer
- By type and size
- By location

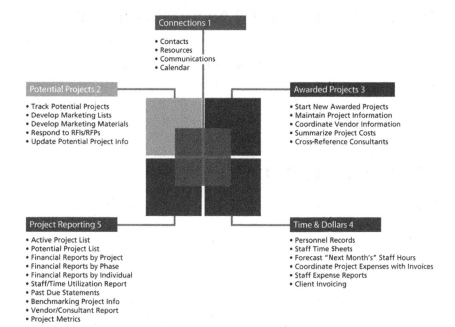

Diagram of our internal project and financial management system.
*We call the system LINK5—linking the five parts of our business process:
connections; potential projects; awarded projects; reporting and metrics; and
time and dollars.*

PROJECT SETUP FOR A POTENTIAL PROJECT

When a potential project is identified, we need basic information in the system
so we can track our progress and success rate. The form in the system is as
follows:

PROJECT SETUP FOR AN AWARDED PROJECT

If we are successful in winning an assignment, we add additional information about the contract type, fee, and additional contacts for billing and reimbursables. If we will be managing the billing, fee receipt, and payment of other consultants, we add each firm's key contact information plus an amount, billed to the client, for overseeing the contractual process.

PROJECT CLOSE-OUT

If the close-out process does not happen soon after the project is finished, it will never happen.

While the close-out information is not critical to running your business, it is critical for your marketing team when responding to RFPs or making new pitches. As your firm grows, it is very difficult to remember everything about all the projects. Having the information in a database makes it much easier to recall.

TIME CAN BE YOUR BEST FRIEND OR YOUR WORST ENEMY

After the first year or two when you have a few tax periods completed, the focus usually turns to "How do I make more money?"

There are a number of ways to make more money. You can:

1. Bring in more business
2. Charge more for your services
3. Reduce your expenses
4. Develop additional services
5. Hire less expensive staff
6. Improve technology
7. Train staff to be more knowledgeable and efficient
8. Improve project workflow

Of these options, #7 and #8 have the potential to provide the greatest and longest-term savings and benefits. I would certainly not eliminate looking at the other options and implementing any of the easier options.

Continuous, on-the-job general training, using staff as mentors, usually beats more specific training. Part of this training process is also continual improvement on form design—that is, forms designed from your client's point of view rather than your firm's point of view. Clear, concise form design saves time.

Streamlining project workflow procedures to reduce churn is perhaps the easiest way to return the most dollars to the bottom line. It is not always possible to set the schedule and workflow since there are many others who have a say in what happens, but when you can influence the process through schedule control, your chances of increasing your profits are the greatest.

Schedule control must start at the presentation phase. Schedules should be prepared and presented from the client's point of view. Tell the client why you need them and when you need them. Tell the client when the other consultants need to be on board and be proactive about creating the list of potential firms, RFPs, and scheduling of interviews.

Time is the one thing we can control at very little or no cost. The value of every hour saved goes right to the bottom line, as every hour wasted reduces the profit. There are many things we do on every project to manage time and protect profitability.

Contract—Make sure each project staff member reads the contract and is aware of the fee, overall schedule, services to be provided, and other firms to coordinate our work with.

Schedule—Make sure each project staff member is aware of the schedule and agrees to the time allocated to do the tasks they are responsible for.

Research—Make sure that the tasks requiring additional research are identified. Work completed without all the necessary information may need to be redone.

Consultants—Make sure that all consultants are on board as soon as possible. It does not cost any more to get the consultants on board early. Churn happens when consultants come on board after work has begun and changes need to be made.

Handoffs—Architecture is like a relay race. There are handoffs of information both internally as well as externally. Sloppy handoffs, where not all the decisions have been made, cause churn for both groups.

Storyboarding—Before starting a phase, create a little storyboard of the activities you need to accomplish, listing the things to remember, the points of coordination with others, and the special details that may require the input of others. A storyboard is like a checklist of things you do not want to forget.

Project Management—If your firm is the architect as well as project manager, there is no excuse if things do not happen when you want them to happen.

If, on the other hand, there is an owner's rep or PM, then I usually say the first one in with the ideas wins. As the architect, you do not want others telling you how or when or what to present. You do not want to do a task that you know you will have to be redone just because the schedule says it is time to do something. You never want someone between you and the client, presenting your ideas in a meeting.

If you manage tasks as they happen, not after the time is up, time will be on your side. Trying to manage tasks after they happen is like swimming upstream. It is not realistic to think you will make up the time in another phase.

Close-Out—Take a few minutes after the project is complete to review how you all spent your time in each phase. Check the hours against forecasted hours. Draw a chart showing the phase(s) where churn occurred and discuss the best way to avoid it on the next project.

DO NOT TRY TO TRICK THE STAFF

Some owners keep all financial information private and do not share either project profitability or firm profitability with the staff. That is OK to do, but be careful when you mention project profitability or project losses.

I have worked for a few firms that kept financial information private but also wanted the staff to *think* things were tight and projects were not profitable. Trying to trick the staff into thinking projects and the firm were not making money is very shortsighted—unless it is true and the staff should be properly informed and be part of the solution to do better next time.

Once staff starts to doubt what management is saying about the finances, they can easily put together enough facts to counter the false information. This is not a good way to solicit positive working relationships, and it can really backfire on the company.

People always ask, "What's the best way to resolve the employee issue of tracking hours worked vs. hours paid vs. hours charged to a project?"

- Tracking an individual's hours worked helps management assess initiative, drive, and dedication. Working excess hours is not a good measure of an individual's performance. We do not encourage employees to work excessive hours.
- Unless a person is part-time, the firm does not track and report on hours paid. An individual's compensation is part base salary, part benefits, and part bonus.
- Total hours spent on a project help management make better decisions when estimating future work. The hours charged to a project do not determine profitability.

There are firms that say projects are not profitable because the hours actually charged to the project exceed the contract projection. Staff take these comments to imply they were either not efficient or not experienced with the project type, or were incorrectly charging their time. This is not good for morale.

First, if the hours worked exceed the hours calculated in the contract, it may be more management's failings than staff failings. It could be that:

- management went in with too low a fee
- the project scope was not fully understood
- the process the firm used in running the project was not efficient and resulted in a lot of churn
- the wrong people were assigned to the project
- the project type was different from usual for the firm and there was a high learning curve to be successful

If more hours were being charged to the project than were allocated and staff was only being paid for 40 hours per week, this is a "paper loss," not a "business loss," and should be reported properly.

Second, this is precisely why it is important for management to include others when preparing a proposal. Let us look at project profitability and firm profitability separately, as the two are different.

PROJECT PROFITABILITY

There are a number of factors that determine if a project will be profitable.

- Negotiating appropriate contract terms, including the initial fee and reimbursables, and understanding the potential for charging for extras or change orders
- Accurate estimating of the time required to do the contracted scope
- Charging the appropriate hourly rates (including benefits) of the staff assigned
- Planning the project steps in storyboard form to avoid churn— educating the client if they have little experience in doing this type of work
- Selecting the other consultants that work well with your firm and determining their scope of work

There is a lot to know and do to be profitable. You can do this on a time or dollar basis.

The Time formula for determining project profitability is simple:
Total hours anticipated per phase – actual hours spent per phase x total fees (excluding reimbursables) – value of the total hours paid to employees (excluding reimbursables) = project profit

The formula for determining FAKE project profitability is also simple:
Total fees (excluding reimbursables – value of the total hours charged to project (excluding reimbursables) = project profit

It is possible to have the best of both worlds when dealing with staff and projects. I think it is beneficial to have key staff involved in estimating the time required for each phase. Staff buy-in is important when determining scope and overall project schedule.

If you use general or average billing rates based on title, then it's OK to have that information somewhat public—to PMs and up. If your company uses actual staff hourly rates as project billing rates, then you might want to keep the rates private. It is important to try to keep salary information private, even though people might be able to figure it out.

FIRM PROFITABILITY

It is important to limit information about firm finances and profitability figures to a few key employees. When we review reporting in the next section, I will discuss key reports that will help you run your business.

It is important to have instructions to staff for preparing timesheets. Here are a few standard instructions most firms follow:

- Full-time billable staff should enter an average of 8 hours/day
- Meetings with reps on general issues should be logged to Research and Development (R&D)
- Meetings with reps on project issues should be logged to project number
- Staff is allowed 16 hours per year for out-of-office general R&D—trade shows or factory or showroom visits—to be approved in advance.
- No limit on out-of-office visits for project-specific R&D
- Travel—if travel to a client takes more than two hours round-trip, charge half to project and half to general administration
- If travel is less than one hour round-trip, charge to project
- Training—AutoCAD, Revit, and general systems training, charge to general office

Tracking billing and general office metrics visually works well for most architectural firms. There are many different ways firms add detail to these charts using Excel or products like Deltek.

Monthly Planner for Project Managers	2/27	3/6	3/13	3/20	3/27	4/3	4/10	4/17
Bill Bailey								
17001C • BCD Taste Tester 2017	8.00	8.00	8.00	8.00	8.00	8.00	8.00	8.00
17001B • BCD Taste Tester 2017 General	24.00	24.00	24.00	24.00	24.00	24.00	24.00	24.00
15124A • Cherry Valley	4.00	4.00	4.00	4.00	4.00	4.00	4.00	4.00
88886 • Professional R&D	8.00	9.00	10.00					
	44.00	45.00	46.00	36.00	36.00	36.00	36.00	36.00
Tom Roberts								
16152 • Pacific 201 M7 Lobby Signage & Branding	1.00							
16094CO3 • Pacific 901 5th Floor DCO #3	2.00							
16085A1 • Pacific 901 8th Floor Test Layouts Add	1.00							
16147 • Pacific 901 Main 3rd & 4th Fl Conf Rooms	1.00	1.00	1.00	2.00	1.00	1.00	1.00	1.00
16125 • Pacific 901 Main 3rd thru 5th Fl Lighting at	1.00							
17002 • Pacific Boston One Financial Center 11th Fl	4.00	4.00	6.00	16.00	8.00			
15045A1F • Pacific Company / DC Add 1 Furniture	1.00							
15045A1 • Ridgeway Company / DC Addendum 1	1.00							
15045G • Pine Tree Company / DC Implementation	3.00	3.00	2.00	3.00	2.00	3.00	2.00	3.00
16132 • Ridgeway Two Armstrong 2nd Fl II	4.00							
99992 • Personal	16.00							
99991 • Vacation	8.00							
	43.00	8.00	9.00	21.00	11.00	4.00	3.00	4.00
Charlie West								
16120 • Airboat Advisors Relocation	8.00							
16120F • Airboat Advisors Relocation Furniture	8.00	8.00						
16151 • Roberts / 100 Bloomingdale / Design	2.00	2.00	2.00	2.00	2.00	2.00	2.00	2.00
16118A • Roberts Design Implementation	6.00	6.00	8.00	12.00	12.00	12.00		
16092 • Epsilon	12.00	14.00	12.00	14.00	4.00	4.00	4.00	4.00
17008 • ANDR 1 Bank St 9th Fl	1.00	1.00						
16026 • ANDR 100 & 200 FSP Lobby Designs	1.00	4.00						
16031 • ANDR Bank St Cafe Upgrades	3.00							
17013 • ANDR Metro Center 4S & 5N RR Finishes	1.00							
16110 • ANDR Metro Center Lobby Refurbishment	1.00	4.00	4.00	1.00	1.00	1.00		
88886 • Professional R&D		12.00						
	43.00	51.00	26.00	29.00	19.00	19.00	6.00	6.00

PART VII

Closing Thoughts

CHAPTER 14

Spectacular Failures

Not everything I have tried over the years worked as planned, and some things I tried did not even work at all. Fortunately, none of my "Big Three" failures was expensive; however, each bruised my ego because I could not make the idea stick. There is a book I wished I had read and now recommend to others to avoid failures like mine. Chip Heath and Dan Heath are the authors. It's called *Made to Stick—Why Some Ideas Survive and Others Die.* The book presents very clearly why some ideas take hold and others do not, and how we can improve our chances.

The ideas we have and the presentations we make to share our ideas should be a series of stories telling people about our approach to business, our goals and objectives, and most specifically how we try to improve our clients' projects. Had I presented each of these ideas as stories, I think they may have been better received.

These are three of my biggest "big idea" failures—there were others. I still think each is a good idea and hope I get the chance to present them again.

BLUEPRINT FOR SAVINGS

In the early years, we worked with building owners and their realtors in preparing test fits for prospective tenants. The hope was that the test fit would move the negotiation along so the company would sign a lease. I have always felt if the owner changed the leasing process, they could get tenants in faster and paying rent sooner. I believe owners and their realtors think of the leasing process as a series of independent tasks rather than each task being an integral part of a singular process. Most prospective tenants make four passes through a building before they actually make the decision to sign a lease.

- **1st Pass—Market survey**
  Client's realtor prepares a listing of available properties.

- **2nd Pass—Decision makers walk through and create short list**
  Owners should have a building comparative checklist to fill in location, parking, image, quality of common areas, building amenities, and costs.
- **3rd Pass—Architect prepares a test fit for each building**
  Building owner should have an architectural information package ready for the tenant's architect including dimensionally accurate floor plan(s) and a building section showing ceiling heights, window and column spacing, accurate core and mechanical drawings, suggested ceiling grid, and furniture symbols. Whichever building owner gets the plans and information to the architect first is the one the architect starts on and spends the most time on.
- **4th Pass—Attorney initiates lease negotiation**
  Building owners should have a lease abstract filled in with first offer terms, ready to discuss all major points of negotiation. If these discussions took place face to face, they could be done in a few days for most situations. Draft leases could follow.

If these simple ideas were followed, rent commencement for most leases could be almost two months earlier.

TEMPLATE FOR THE PERFECT RFP

It seems obvious that if a company wants to have effective competitive bidding for an architectural project, they need to have a good RFP they can send out to firms. Herein lies the problem. Most RFPs do not include sufficient information about the project for the architect to define their services and thereby calculate their fee. What actually happens is that the client/representative sends out an RFI (Request for Information), not an RFP. The RFI has questions for the architect about the firm, its history, and size and types of projects, yet very little information is given about the proposed project. However, they still expect the architect to send back a proposal describing scope and proposed fee.

This led me to develop a standard approach to the RFP process. The client/representative could use the format simply by checking off boxes of the services they wanted the architect to include in their response. I drafted what I hoped would be the perfect RFP—just what architects would like to receive.

The RFP template included five parts:

1. Information the client could fill in about their current situation
   - Current location
   - How long they have been at this location
   - Amount of USF/RSF
   - Total number of existing workplaces, including offices
   - Total number of workplaces and offices occupied at time of move-in
   - Total number of workplaces and offices currently occupied, including a copy of floor plans
2. Information the client could fill in about their project goals
   - Reason for renovating/relocating/building a new building
   - Do they have a new location in mind?
   - Do they have a desired image?
   - What message would they like to send to staff and customers about their brand/growth/workplace strategy/green initiatives/efficiency/image?
   - Do they have a budget guideline (low/middle/high), and what's included?
   - What are they looking for in an architect?
     - Creativity
     - Experience with similar type projects/similar type clients
     - Great references
     - Partner participation
     - A team that shows excitement and creativity and is fun to work with
   - In addition, a section about insurance, liability, etc.
3. Information the architect could fill in about their company
   - Company background
   - Project approach
   - Proposed team
   - Proposed fee—using enclosed chart
4. Description of proposed scope of services
   For each phase, the template includes all the possible services architects normally provide. Next to each is a box that the client/

representative checks if that is a service they desire. Using this approach, the desired scope of work is very clear to all bidders:

- Preleasing
- SD/DD/CD documentation
- Bidding/Construction observation
- Move–In/Close-Out
- Set up for facilities management—Day 2 Work

5. Information about the scope of services provided by the PM/ owner's rep, if there is one:

- Prepare/Update schedule weekly, run all meetings, send out meeting notes
- Set project budget categories—what's in and what's not
- Maintain project schedule—schedule client involvement
- Send out RFPs to other consultants, negotiate contracts, manage invoices/payments
- Send out RFPs to furniture, A/V, IT, Security, Mover, other vendors—level bids
- Send out RFPs to CMs—level bids

When I finished the template, I sent it out to about 100 firms: realtors, owner's reps, project managers, and to some former clients.

After reading *Made to Stick*, I know what I did wrong in my presentation and will send it out again another day because it is a very important subject.

My cover letter was as follows:

March 21, 2007

Transparency is a WIN WIN for all.

Over the past 27 years, CPG has tried to continuously improve its service through new ways of working, using improved technology and better-trained and informed staff to keep "raising the bar" and improving service levels to all of our clients.

We have been asked by many to recommend ways to change the RFP and Architectural selection process to be much clearer for realtors and clients to understand, clarify and compare the responses provided by Architectural firms.

Today the scope of services and corresponding fees for potential projects is not at all **transparent** and clients **often pay more than they expect** for services when relocating or renovating their workplace.

This is mainly due to two reasons: First, there is usually an incomplete "definition of what is needed" in the RFP. This results in each firm preparing their response on assumed understanding of the desired scope of work. Second, there is not a way to easily compare providers' scope of services and associated fees.

To accomplish this transparency, CPG has created a standard **"Scope Document"**, a **"Standard RFP"** and a **"Standard Scorecard"** that can be used by all. We hope this approach will promote: Honesty = Transparency = Predictability = Stability and Better Value for the Client.

This approach will also improve the quality of competition, provide for more comprehensive and appropriate services as well as manage the level of fee variance to the client. **A WIN WIN for all!**

Please look over what we have prepared. Share this with your colleagues, friends, and even our competitors. Tell us what you think. We look forward to your comments.

For a free copy of the RFP, please email gary_unger@cpgarch.com or for feedback give me a call at 203-967-3456.

I even developed a scorecard to help clients score and select the firm that best meets their needs.

Guess how many responses I got.

Zero.

I was so caught up with my brilliant idea, I forgot to use some basic Marketing 101 principles.

First, I should have spelled out that there are a number of audiences that could benefit from a standard approach to writing an RFI or RFP—clients, architects, owner's reps/project managers, and realtors.

I sent my package to the wrong audience. Had I sent it first to architects, I may have gotten some traction—they are the real beneficiaries who best understand the need. I then could have seeded the idea with the others.

Second, I should have prepared a white paper for each group explaining the problem I saw and the benefits to working together to find a better approach to selecting a firm.

Third, I should have requested comments and incorporated them in a draft document. Mine looked too final.

Even though it was a total bust, I occasionally get calls from people saying they need to prepare an RFP and they heard I had a good template.

What I thought would be a win-win was a lose-lose.

I'm sure I will take a second look at this subject in the future and try harder the next time to include others.

STANDARD DOCUMENTS

Similar to my desire to develop a standard RFP/RFI, I thought about approaching the subject of office standards with other architects.

When a new person is hired in any architectural firm, they need to be trained in the special way drawings are set up, specs written, documents saved, and forms used. I proposed an approach similar to the "open source code app" that programmers use.

My idea was to identify processes and procedures that all firms could use in a similar way. I started by listing the things we do over and over again that are not part of our firm's branding and marketing plans.

These are some of the forms most firms use on a regular basis.

When I started the firm, I produced a complete set of coordinated forms and templates used for marketing purposes, project management, and presentations. These have been improved significantly over the years and could be shared with others:

	Word	Excel
Administrative Forms		
Agenda	X	
CD Drawing Release	X	
Confidentiality Agreement: Client	X	
Confidentiality Agreement: Vendor	X	
Indemnification Clause	X	
Meeting Minutes	X	
Memorandum	X	

	Word	Excel
RFPs and Contracts		
Acoustical Consultant	X	
AV Consultant	X	
Civil Consultant	X	
CM Consultant	X	
Furniture Consultant	X	
IT Consultant	X	
Kitchen Consultant	X	
Landscape Consultant	X	
MEP Consultant	X	
MEP Bid Comparison		X
Moving Consultant	X	
Project Manager/Owners Rep	X	
PM/Owners Bid Comparison		X
Structural Consultant	X	
RFP—Award Letters	X	
(for each type of consultant)		
RFP—Reject Letters	X	
(for each type of consultant)		
Pre-Leasing Forms		
Accessibility Checklist—CT, NY	X	
Accessibility Compliance Report	X	
ADA .PDF Checklist	X	
Building Code Compliant Checklist	X	
Building Information for Permit	X	
Building and Zoning Analysis	X	
Building Area Analysis		X
Building Comparison Checklist		X
Building Owner Response		X
Facility Evaluation		X
Field Survey Checklist		X
Key Activities Checklist	X	
Preliminary Client Schedule		X
Preliminary Code Compliance	X	

	Word	Excel
Personnel and Space—short form		X
Pre-Leasing Budget		X
Preliminary Project Schedule		X
Site Checklist		X
Site Survey checklist		X
Tenant Workletter	X	X

Schematic Design Forms

Budgets		
Preliminary Construction Budget		X
Preliminary Branding Budget		X
Preliminary Furniture Budget		X
Personnel and Space—Long Form		X
Schedules		
Overall Time Line		X
Client Schedule		X
Consultant Schedule		X
Surveys	X	
AV	X	
Equipment	X	
IT/Technology	X	
Furniture	X	

Design Development Forms

Artwork Budget		X
IT/Technology Budget		X

CD Forms and Templates

CD Architectural Checklist		X
CD MEP Checklist		X
Final Code Compliance	X	
Update Furniture Specs		X
Trade Coordination Checklist	X	
Interior Specs	X	

	Word	Excel
Construction Observation Forms		
CM Bid Comparison		X
Trade Bid Comparison		X
Change Proposal Request	X	
Construction Schedule	X	
Base Building Punch List		X
Exterior Punch List		X
Field Order/Bulletin	X	
Furniture Punch List		X
Interior Building Checklist	X	X
Long Lead Items Checklist		X
Utility Punch List		X
Addendum	X	
Clarification	X	
Definitions of Bid/Contract Terms	X	
RFI Response	X	
Shop Drawing Log		X
Supplemental Instructions	X	
Move Coordination Forms and Templates		
Cleaning Guidelines	X	
Employee Move Instructions	X	
Employee Move Ticket	X	
Close-Out Forms and Templates		
Architect Project Close-Out	X	
Client Project Close-Out	X	
Consultant Contract Close-Out	X	

They all have headers and are ready for each firm to add their logo. All are modifiable for specific use.

What I later determined was that each firm was so protective of their work that the idea of sharing was out of the question. Creating standard documents was not a bad idea, just poorly presented.

CHAPTER 15

Nagging Concerns

EDUCATION

This is certainly *top* on my list of things that need to happen both in school and in the office. I feel architecture schools need to weave in Professional Practice throughout the five or six years and not just count on a one-semester course as being sufficient.

Graduates need to know much more about the practice to have any chance of getting ahead in the real world within a reasonable period of time. There needs to be an easy way to introduce many of the subjects along with semester assignments.

Firms should have continuing professional practice education as part of each project. Even if an employee is starting out doing basic detailing, they should be exposed to all the forms being used on the project. The mentoring program referred to earlier is a perfect way to introduce new topics.

Employees taking the management route vs. the design route should avail themselves of any outside business courses the firm is willing to contribute to. There are the online lynda.com courses or the Kahn Academy courses that are very easy to follow on many subjects.

One of the things we practice is the one-minute "elevator pitches" on various subjects. These work wonders for quick pitches and give staff knowledge and confidence when talking to others.

FLEETING SERVICES

I touched on this subject in an earlier chapter, but it is worth mentioning again. Architects seem to be left at the starting blocks whenever new design concepts and practice strategies are introduced. Most recently, the hot topics have been workplace strategy, space utilization, and the transition to collaborative space design.

WORKPLACE STRATEGY

Before architects had time to blink, they found workplace strategy consulting firms coming out of the woodwork. All of a sudden, realtors, owner's reps, and furniture manufacturers have experts writing articles and giving free seminars on the subject. A few of the larger architectural firms were on top of the subject and quickly hired workplace strategists, but for the average size architectural firm, it is hard to market against free consulting offered by others.

PROGRAMMING

Programming used to be a major part of architects' preliminary project work, but today many of the real estate and project management firms have "space calculators" on their websites. Although most lack the correct formulas to add circulation to get to usable square feet and a proper add-on percentage to get from usable to rentable, they are up and available. Gone are the days when architects spent hours working with departments to determine their adjacency requirements, interdepartmental workflow, and filing needs. Today, filing cabinets are nonexistent in most offices.

LONG-RANGE PLANNING

Who does it anymore? Architects are now told the company needs so many offices of certain sizes; so many workstations and depending on the functions, the architect will calculate conference room needs. Enclaves and semiprivate work areas, open lounge areas, and cafés are calculated by population. Determining space requirements for alternative officing, touchdown, and hoteling spaces are calculated differently for each company based on their HR policies. Transparent glass walls, marker walls, or movable walls are the trend today, and flexibility is key. Furniture that is flexible, tables that go up and down, and lighting and HVAC controlled by the individual are all part of the new interior package. Planning for future needs is managed by having flexible work hours, alternative officing policies, and work-at-home plans. While the amount of total space leased is reduced for many firms, the average USF or RSF per employee is less.

RENTABLE AREA CALCULATIONS

This is a service I am personally pleased to say is now out of favor. There was a time when we were asked to measure the landlord's space to determine if the number used in a lease or purchase document was calculated correctly. The chance that two firms measured a building the same way is slim to none especially when the method used is the REBNY (Real Estate Board of New York) method. The only accurate way to compare the utilization of space in buildings is by measuring the usable area according to the BOMA (Building Owners and Managers Association) method. Now, how architects assist their clients in evaluating and comparing space in various buildings is to compare the actual USF.

COST BUDGETING/ESTIMATING

Instead of the architect estimating potential construction costs, GCs and CMs provide this service, much of the time for free. These preconstruction estimates are prepared based on conceptual architectural plans with no MEP, AV, security, or IT indicated. For this reason, there is a lot of guesswork in terms of scope and quality, often causing early estimates to be higher than expected. No one wants to be embarrassed later when final plans are prepared, so it is normal for estimates to be high in the early phases to cover all sorts of unforeseen development.

PROJECT MANAGEMENT

The key to a well-run project is the way the client is advised and kept in the loop.

Traditionally, the architect provided this management service as part of their overall architectural service. The success of their management service translated directly to the profitability of the project. *One would hope that the project managers within the architect's office are tuned to the internal process and are able to maintain the day-to-day contact with the client.*

Beginning in early 2000, clients started outsourcing project management to reduce costs. Many architects missed the chance to pull out project management from their typical service offering and make it a specialty. Realtors, owner's reps, and project management firms now sell their services to clients from a risk-avoidance basis. They say, "If you don't have someone following the project for you the costs or schedule could get out of line. You need someone *on your side* looking after your needs."

The presumption is made that the fee paid to the consultant will be more than offset by the reduction in the architects' fee. This is partially true. The architect is forced to lower their fee, but in reality, the architect must still have a PM on the project to coordinate with the clients PM so there are no significant savings for the architect—just less fee.

Sometimes an extra set of eyes is beneficial, but sometimes an extra body can get in the way, especially if the architect has to go through a PM to get to the client.

These are just a few of the services that the profession has lost. The services most easily plucked from the architect of course are those that have little to no liability associated with them.

CHAPTER 16

My Two Best Jobs

CAUDILL ROWLETT SCOTT (CRS): 1968–1974

Who wouldn't want Bill Caudill to be their architect? What a *smile*. He was the most personable guy I ever worked for, and he had a manner of speaking where you just wanted to follow him everywhere. We always hear about the three most important things when making a presentation: your appearance, how you speak, and what you say. Bill was great at all three!

A couple of West Texas boys founded Caudill Rowlett Scott (CRS), in the late '40s. Both Bill Caudill and John Rowlett were professors at Texas A&M University. They were later joined by Wally Scott and became a powerhouse firm that received many significant national awards, and finally through a number of acquisitions, they are now a part of HOK Architects.

For me, CRS was the best firm I had ever worked for, and I patterned all of the great things we did and still do after my experiences at CRS Architects, American Express (my next job), and Gensler. I never worked for Gensler but have followed owners Art, Ed, and David forever and have always been impressed with everything they do. They are remarkable to have stayed at the top of the pack since the firm's inception.

When CRS Architects opened an NYC office in 1968, I made a beeline to work for them. They were in an expansion mode and within a few years opened offices around the country. The three leaders in the NYC office were Chuck Thomsen, Norman Hoover, and Jack Smith. They were all partners in the firm, all transferred from Houston. They were young, full of energy, tremendously creative, and fabulous to work for. The New York office thrived and grew on their energy.

I was part of a very young design team. We were all feisty and very sure of ourselves. People like Fred Preiss, Peter Piven, and Peter Gumpel were so talented and continually challenged the younger ones like me to perform well beyond our capabilities. Our offices were at 230 Park Avenue, on the sixth floor. My drafting table was just one window to the left of the big clock facing up Park Avenue. My view was mesmerizing. The office atmosphere was special. None of the leaders ever had to say, "Would you please do something?" Somehow, everyone knew what needed to be done and pitched in as if it were their own firm.

We were professional disruptors.

I remember one Friday Chuck and Jack were talking about a major potential client coming in for a new business presentation on Monday. I decided that the lobby looked pretty shabby and worn, so I bought a gallon of paint and gave it a fresh coat on Saturday. Another guy was already in on Saturday giving the kitchen a real cleaning, and another came in that afternoon to clean up the conference rooms and rehang the photos.

We all wanted the firm to make a good impression. I have no recollection whether or not we got that potential client, but I do remember this happened often. It takes so little effort to take pride in where you work—and believe me, it was appreciated by Jack and Chuck.

In my second year at CRS, my career took a dramatic turn. I always knew I was not as good a designer as others were, and admitting it was very hard. Everyone believes the words *architect* and *designer* are synonymous and the words *architect* and *manager* are opposites. I knew one day I would be getting a call saying, "We want you to focus on management." That call came. Through chats with Chuck, Norman, and Jack I shifted gears and became exclusively involved with client project management. This turning point was tough to acknowledge, but I could quickly see the improvement in my attitude and my performance, and fortunately, I really liked it. It was easy for me.

CRS had all the best professional practice policies I had ever heard of at the time or have been exposed to since. Each of the offices was set up administratively as a profit center, and as such there was constant pressure from "Houston" about our project/office profitability. If you read Art Gensler's book, *Art's Principles*, he says that one of the reasons for their success was the "One Firm—Firm" idea, where all offices work together for the common good and are not competitive. In spite of this, CRS was a very successful firm.

One of the funniest and most talented people in the office was Peter Gumpel. He was both a superb designer and a great project manager. He was one of the few who did not have to make the decision I did as to which road to go down, designer or project manager—he could do it all perfectly.

Each month, Peter complained bitterly when "Houston" told us that our projects were losing money. Peter figured it out: He said, "Let's not record all the hours we worked on projects—only those hours we get paid for—eight hours a day." We all worked crazy hours and never thought twice about recording *all* our time each week on every project. We recorded all our hours because we were proud of how hard we worked and wanted "Houston" to know it. Lo and behold, when we changed the way we entered our project time, the profitability of the projects and profit of the office sharply increased.

Be straight with your employees when you talk about project profitability. All hours should be recorded properly to use when estimating time for the next similar project and for calculating the fee. Owners should not say the project is losing money if it is not.

Now for the Best Part of CRS

CRS had the best client working concepts of any firm I worked for. Their process was not only fresh and creative, but always took into account the best interest of the client. There were many ideas that sped up the process, assured good design, and assured repeat business. Most important, the process reduced task churn and assured adherence to the schedule.

The four principal ideas from CRS that I used when I started my own business were:

- Programming
- Squatters
- Snow Cards
- "Fast Track"

Programming

Willie Pena was a Partner in CRS Houston and developed the original methodology for determining a company's personnel, space, and special area needs. His approach was called Problem Seeking, and his book was recently republished by HOK Architects.

Willie developed the "program of needs" visually, not numerically, and indicated not only the number and size of spaces, but also took into account the relationships between spaces. Color coordinating the program spaces worked well to easily understand needs, adjacencies, and special relationships.

I used these programming concepts at American Express in 1974 when planning their first headquarters building, then again after I left American Express and was called back in 1982 to do the programming, stacking, and blocking for their second headquarters at the World Financial Tower.

Squatters

CRS had an excellent reputation in designing schools, colleges, and universities throughout the country. Most of the clients were located in cities and states too far for the team to travel back and forth in a day, so Bill Caudill designed the following solution.

This quote is from Bill Caudill about the Blackwell project:

> Because of the long commute between the project site and the firm's office, a lot of time, energy, money, and ideas were wasted. To conquer this problem, the partners set up a temporary office and "squatted" at the school site until all the design issues with the school board were resolved. This idea was so effective that CRS incorporated it in all their future projects.

The goal was to end the week with programming and SD approved. Not only was this a very efficient and profitable process, but the client was also fully engaged, loved the approach, and rarely made significant concept changes after approval. What started as a way of working out of necessity became a desired procedural approach and a major selling feature for the firm.

Snow Cards

The first day of every squatter's week was spent making ourselves available to all the staff to understand their needs. In most cases, the project was educational work, so it was teachers, professors, and school administrators who would drop in on us. We would take over a classroom or large conference room for the week and ask each of those who dropped in to write on a 5x7 index card whatever was on their mind regarding the project. It was impromptu and very effective. Many staff members returned a few times during the week as they thought of other ideas they wanted us to consider.

We pinned up subject headings around the room. Each card was to contain only one thought, and they could be as diverse as lighting, acoustics, furniture, colors, materials, functional adjacencies, mechanical, air quality, desire for natural light, and electrical needs. By the end of the week, when the client came in for the presentation and viewed the cards that were pinned to the walls by categories, they were so pleased that we took their ideas to heart, someone on the CRS team coined the phrase "we snowed them"—thus the phrase *snow cards*.

By the end of the first day, the walls were covered with cards, which gave us great design direction for the development of the program and architectural concepts.

I learned many valuable lessons from participating in these squatters:

- Most clients love to participate in the process; you just need to have the proper forum
- Clients like that you listen and use their ideas
- It is very easy to find ways to have something for everyone in the program
- There is no downside to having the client participate; only up-side potential
- This squatters/charrette concept is the best way to quickly share valuable ideas

When CPG was selected to design the new headquarters for US Tobacco in Stamford, we used the "snow card" and "squatters" concepts to start the project. Management wanted staff to participate in the relocation process, and this was an easy process to initiate. The team benefited greatly from the ideas that were presented.

Fast Track

The expression *fast track* has been around for a long time, but most people do not know how the expression came about. As it relates to construction and the architectural industry, the expression was coined in 1968. Here's the story:[5]

> In 1968, The New York State University Construction Fund (SUCF) re-tained Caudill Rowlett Scott (CRS) to study ways to shorten schedules. The completed study hypothesized that the SUCF could save 25–45

---

5 "Fast-track building construction," *Wikipedia*, accessed March 5, 2018, https:// en.wikipedia.org/wiki/Fast-track_construction.

percent of the time with phased construction. That is huge. They could stay within their procurement regulations by selecting a company (a CM) for construction management services—who would provide no construction labor or materials—based on qualifications. The CM would do no actual construction work. The CM would have a professional responsibility to represent the owner's best interest as an agent, similar to that of an architect. The CM would advise the architect and owner on cost and construction technology during the design phase and would estimate the total cost. The architect would complete the construction drawings and specifications in phases and the CM would take open, competitive bids for those phases of the work, overlapping the design and construction activities. For instance, the CM might take bids for site clearing and grading as soon as the basic building configuration was set and drawings and specifications for that phase of the work were complete. Companies that typically functioned as subcontractors would bid the work. The low bidder would have a direct contract with the owner, metamorphosing from subcontractor to prime contractor. The owner would have multiple prime contracts.

The author of this process was Chuck Thomsen of CRS. The New York office of CRS designed and managed the construction of a number of schools on Long Island for SUCF using the Fast Track process. These preengineered one-story schools were built much faster and for less cost than a traditional school. They were very popular in meeting capacity crises in many school districts. The process was so successful that it was then used on many of CRS's other projects, even when the preengineered component was not utilized.

The lesson learned was that the expression *fast track* only works when there is a positive plan in place, accepted by the client, architect, and contractor, to overlap the phases of work to get the same amount of work done in a shorter period of time.

Today many clients, project managers, and owner's reps talk about the need to "go fast" but do not set up the controls and processes to take advantage of the potential savings. Going fast without securing proper approvals causes churn, resulting in additional cost and time. Fast track is not about working longer hours to increase the profit.

My six years with CRS were special because management trusted the staff to perform. There was no babysitting or hand-holding. If you did not or could not perform, you were out. Looking back, the entire office was a group of over-achievers who liked to work together.

I was 26 when I joined CRS. The idea that they trusted me to visit a client, sometimes a college president, a Board of Education, or a group of professors, amazed me. I cannot remember ever working harder to prepare the questions I would ask or the answers I would need to have for standard questions.

I learned a lesson at CRS that became critical later when I worked for American Express: if you do not know the answer to a question, don't try to fudge or talk your way out of it. Just say I do not know and will find out as soon as possible.

When project goals were set, the teams had a lot of flexibility to design the best approach for the client. The principals talked a lot about managing expectations—both client and firm expectations and trying to align the needs of both to end up with a strong solution.

AMERICAN EXPRESS: 1974–1980

In 1974, a friend suggested I interview for the job of "Managing the Planning and Design" for the new 1.2 million-square-foot American Express Headquarters at the tip of Manhattan, at 125 Broad Street. I had never interviewed with a corporation, so I had no idea what to do, how to prepare, or, for that matter, what to wear. I had a lot of hesitation of leaving, because CRS was so good to me.

I must have passed the first round because I was asked to come in for a second meeting with the head of the real estate group. As luck would have it, his VP attended the meeting, and I found out as we chatted before the interview that he also lived in Greenwich. That broke the ice, and I went from shaking in my boots to just fidgeting. From then on, the meeting went well. I knew I did not have the experience or qualifications for the job, so when asked how I would approach the management of the project, I used as an example the way I managed educational projects for CRS. I had never worked on a school project as large as 1.2 million square feet, but I thought all the schools I worked on must have added up to more than that.

Lesson learned—If asked what kind of similar experience you have and your answer starts with "Well, I don't . . ."—you will probably not survive for another round. Rather, if your answer starts with "I have had similar experiences; let me tell you about them," you might make it through.

That is the first thing that came to mind, and I blurted it out. There was no way I could fake my way into claiming I had any high-rise NYC building experience. I knew nothing about corporate organizational structures and could not even say I had an American Express card, used their Travelers Cheques, or made travel reservations at an Amex Travel office. I was really out of my element.

I used every metaphor I could think of having to do with campus planning and how that related directly to corporate planning. I talked about the different fields: architecture, sciences, engineering, humanities, etc., and that while each school often occupied their own building, the process for determining needs, defining space, setting standards, preparing layouts, and getting faculty approval would be similar to designing department spaces in one building.

I even made the dumb statement that if you stacked up all the schools on a campus, it would be like a high-rise building and then tried to make the point that campus planning might in fact be harder. They had my number all the way along but played on with me and cut me short before I surely would have self-destructed. I got the job.

They later said they liked the way I handled myself, and, while I was totally panicked, I must have looked like I was at ease with them.

I have always said, "How could I pass up an opportunity like that?" I was *very inexperienced* in running big projects and told them so in the interview process. I'm not sure what they saw in me, but the fact that they trusted me and knew I would work hard made me feel good.

It was an easy professional decision to make the move, but a very difficult personal one. The CRS team was the best, and Greenwich was just a one-stop train ride from Grand Central, a quick elevator ride up to the 6th floor in 230 Park, and a short walk down the hall. To get downtown to American Express, I had to take a more-than-30-minute hot and steamy subway ride from Grand Central to the Wall Street stop, then had a three block walk to the building. That added about an hour and a half to my daily commute, for a new total of three and a half hours a day. That was a real bummer.

I had planned to spend two years at Amex to complete the headquarters building, then go back to CRS, but after the project was finished, I was asked to stay on and run the Planning and Design Group Worldwide. I did that for five more years. It was a fabulous company with overwhelming projects all over the world. When I was there, they had 3,500 locations of all types in 125 countries. I had a large team but was in the enviable position of deciding which projects I wanted to work on myself—I took England, France, Italy, Canada, and Mexico.

The First Two Years: 1974–1976

American Express purchased the empty shell of a building at 125 Broad Street at the tip of Manhattan from a developer that was foreclosed a year earlier. The finishing of the shell and subsequent relocation of all Amex employees turned out to be the largest nongovernmental move in the history of NYC. Each of the 30,000 SF floors was wide open with no fireproofing, elevators, toilet rooms, mechanical, electrical, plumbing, etc. We had a blank slate to work with.

Selecting and managing the team of consultants was a fabulous experience. We selected ISD as the lead design firm with Bob Fymat as the lead designer and H. L. Lazar as the general contractor. As the youngest one on the project and the one in charge, I sometimes wondered each night as I took the subway uptown what the next day would bring. Working with the unions and the building department in NYC was an eye-popping experience.

Pleasing Division Presidents

One of the most difficult parts of the project was getting all the group presidents—Card, Travel, Travelers Cheques, Bank—and their staff groups to agree on which floors they would occupy. Everyone wanted to be in the top elevator bank with the Amex executives. The advantage I had was that I was new with the company and did not understand the politics, so my recommendations for stacking and blocking were based purely on workflow, projected staffing numbers, special area needs, and floor size. There were four elevator banks, so each bank of floors had different usable areas.

Looking back, I needed to position my comments and recommendations only on facts. If my recommendations drifted to hearsay or "here's what I think," I would have been crushed. I can still hear Dan saying, "Don't bring me problems, bring me solutions."

Dan came to Amex from Ford. He was head of Real Estate there for many years and had a very distinct style. My first impression was that he did not know the first thing about any of my projects—then I quickly realized he not only knew everything that I knew, but much more. He was always very relaxed, looking like he did not have a worry in the world and was ready to go out to play golf.

If I finished a project ahead of schedule, he would say I padded the schedule. If I finished a project under the AR, Appropriation Request, he would say I padded the budget. On the surface there was no winning with Dan, but deep down you knew he respected you—he just liked to play the game of cat and mouse.

The more I thought about Dan's comment of requiring everyone to come in with solutions, not just problems, the more I realized this was the kind of person I wanted to work for.

Lesson Learned: When you bring just problems, you might not be happy having to live with implementing someone else's solution. When you offer solutions to problems, you are in a better position to manage the direction and the outcome.

Floor Assignments

We made the decision early on that it was important in determining floor assignments that each Division base their space needs on staffing projections for the next five years. Even though each Division prepared five-year business plans, they were more like marketing plans describing new products and services. The plans did not include staff or related space projections to accomplish the business goals.

After reading a few of the business plans, I realized that I could provide a very valuable service to the Divisions by learning to translate their marketing plans and business projections to staffing and space requirements. It turned out that it was quite easy to do. Once I determined the activity indicators for each group, I could divide the projections by the indicators and the result would be the number of people required. As the only one on the project team with knowledge of how to calculate space, I was able to persuade the group that my stacking options were the best approach and would cause the least disruption and need to restack over the next few years.

The difficulty I had in getting everyone to agree to my recommendations was not apparent to me at first—*the problem was that none of the groups wanted to be charged for space that was not being used immediately.* Even though the concept of charging departments for the space they occupy is a bit silly, it was a hurdle we had to overcome.

When we decided that the cost of *all growth space* would be absorbed by the real estate department, the Divisions approved their growth projections, space needs, and the building stacking plan. My presentation to management showed that it was far less expensive for the company to absorb the charge for any extra space than it was to bear the costs and disruption of groups having to move every time they added staff or ran out of space.

Thinking back, the speed at which we did all this was impressive, given the only tools our department had were a four-function calculator, a roll of 36-inch-wide brown paper, a typewriter, and access to the secretarial pool's Wang word processing equipment. This was 1974, and I did not get my first computer until 1982, two years after I started CPG Architects. It was an IBM dual floppy machine with far less power than my iWatch.

Visual presentations to the Board were always freehand on brown wrapping paper, usually 3 feet high by 6 feet long, vertically pinned to the boardroom wall, showing options of how the Divisions would be distributed over the 41 floors. To show options, we used sheets of mylar over the brown paper, with colored shapes showing the major distribution of groups. Within a couple of weeks, the stacking and blocking plans were approved, and we were on to design.

Coming Out of the Woodwork

When you run a large project, you realize very quickly how big your decisions are and how many people come out of the woodwork saying they are friends with the chairman, have done work in his house, supplied carpet in his bedroom, or did his landscaping. In all cases, it became important to check them out to separate those who were real from those who were just trying to push their way in.

Unfortunately, the only way to do that was to see everyone. It was also important to learn if there were ideas you should consider. The worst thing would be to turn someone away who had great ideas or products that could really help. Fortunately, in every case, the chairman let us decide which products and services to use. Every decision we made had to be backed up with competitive bids because we knew the entire project was going to be audited. We passed the final audit with flying colors.

This is true even now at CPG. We get so many requests by vendors who say they have great products or service ideas. Many say they know the head of the company we are working for. We must see them all and give everyone a fair chance, as we hope others will give us a fair chance to present our case when we are trying to introduce our firm.

We are frequently surprised and pleased when someone comes in with a great idea. Vendors and manufacturer reps are extremely important to us.

Personnel and Space Projections

For each division and all staff groups, we had to prepare itemized staff lists and space requirements for the designers so they could start preparing test fits for review and approval. The format I set up enabled us to use the existing three- and five-year business projections and, through activity indicator translation, projected staff and special area requirements. Critical to the process was to get each department head to sign off on the projections. The form was designed to be a living document, easily changed as the staffing changed. That way, the groups could participate actively in planning their future needs.

Design Concepts

Before starting the planning for each floor, we held a series of meetings to determine how the staff groups were going to occupy the new building. The groups moving into the building came from many different locations in the City, and some were quite protective of their spaces that they wanted to carry forward to the new building. We needed to make a number of decisions that affected the design of all the floors. Once approved, these standards or guidelines were given to the designers to start preparing plans.

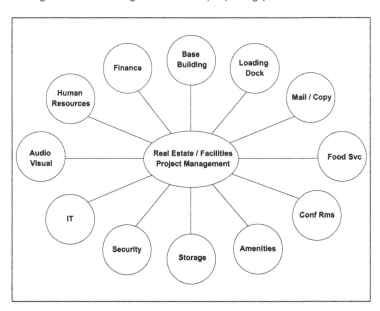

Saying *No*

It is tough to say *no*, especially to someone who may be levels above you. In projects of this size and those even smaller, there is always a date set after which there will be no further floor plan changes. If we did not do this, it would be impossible to get the construction documents prepared and the space built. We all know there are many types of changes; some require plan modifications and others are simple—thus the need to walk a fine line between saying *yes* and saying *no*.

I had a standard answer, no matter who called or what type of change was required. My standard answer has served me well through the years. It was always and still is "Let's get together to understand what you want." The trick is to find a way to say *yes*. It is very easy to say *no* and play the tough person. If things got heated and they dropped the chairman's name, my answer was that we should go up and see him together. That was usually the end to that request. Still, I tried to get everyone's change made because I knew I would have to call in favors sometime in the future.

Metrics Rule

In every line of business, having accurate information readily available is critical to being able to make intelligent decisions. The ability to recall lease data, department metrics, schedule information, and cost data is critical to being able to answer management's questions in a timely fashion. Questions may come when you are in a meeting, on the phone, or standing in front of the chairman, which can be the most difficult. At all times, you need to be able to respond professionally. Management expects facility managers to have a handle on exactly what is going on at all times. This was truly one of the most difficult parts of my job.

Keeping track of data was tough in 1974. We had no personal computers, fax, cell phones, email, or ability to text. We had a four-function calculator, a typewriter, and access to a Wang word processing secretarial pool. We had loads of columnar pads. I always said one day I would build a system so facility managers looked good to management. I ended up doing that, and it is selling well to this day.

My Biggest Surprises

I learned a lot about working with corporate folks during that project. I am sure the folks at Amex, top to bottom, were no different from employees at any other company. To generalize:

- The employees in the *middle ranks* were the toughest to deal with, as they sometimes wanted to impress their bosses by asking for, and in some cases insisting on getting, favors. They often pushed for exceptions to the "level grading system" for office vs. workstation assignments or wanted their department to be on the best side of the building and in the best corner.
- The employees in the *bottom ranks* were the most appreciative. In every case I can think of, they benefited the most from the relocation, even if it was as simple as just being in a clean new building with a functioning HVAC system. Everyone got all new furniture, a full cafeteria, and use of other special spaces that dramatically improved their well-being.
- The employees in the *executive ranks* were fantastic to deal with. They appreciated how hard the task was for the real estate department and always made themselves available for meetings. The division presidents and their staffs were very different from one another, as their businesses were so different. Under one roof were the Card Division, Travel Division, The Amex Bank, Travelers Cheques, and all the staff group offices of Personnel, Accounting, Finance, Administration, Real Estate, Legal, Technology, etc.

The determination of pay grades for all employees was based upon the Hay System, and the points one got were used to determine a number of things, most important, office or workstation sizes. Some may remember that major corporations used the Hay System to evaluate each job description and assign points for responsibility and authority. The points one got were determined by averaging the same job description across many companies. Everyone in Amex was interviewed by a Hay consultant to evaluate his or her job.

I was fortunate that a friend briefed me on how to answer the questions, and I was amazed at how many points I got. I was told to answer each question by saying:

- I have authority to spend . . .
- I have authority to hire . . .
- I have authority to approve . . .
- I have responsibility to . . .

Whatever the question, my answers needed to be an action statement indicating I had approval from management, without asking, to make many decisions that were both financial and procedural. Many people have a lot of responsibility but very little authority to implement. I must have sounded to the interviewer like I was at the level of the chairman. Because of my points, I remember being able to have an office the same size as division presidents.

Lesson learned: Always do your homework before being interviewed.

The most ridiculous request we received was after move-in. An executive's assistant called our office one Monday morning and asked to have a porter come up and pick up some leaves that had fallen off the ficus plants. She was not kidding.

Life after Open House

Unless you have worked for a corporation, you have no idea how difficult it can be for the facilities group to respond to new work after the company has moved into its new digs. After the big party is over and the consultant's work is finished, the internal facility group's work is just beginning. It is tough to respond quickly enough to users' pent-up demands for change. To keep the peace, I established a first in/first out policy. We handled the requests in the order we got them—or at least that is the way people thought we worked. This was my chance to help those who made my life easy during the initial construction. I never imagined or appreciated the number of real estate requests that could be made every day, some of them for pretty inconsequential things.

Here is a sampling of some of the questions:

- How many vacant workstations are available?
- Where can I find space for 10 interns starting in two weeks?
- We need to add an extra-large office in the finance department for a person starting on Monday.
- There is a group uptown whose lease is up, and we want them to move into the headquarters—where can we put them that's close to our department?
- We are promoting five managers to assistant vice presidents, and they need larger workstations.
- Bill is being promoted, and we need VP-level furniture in his office.

- It is too bright in my area; I am hot I am cold.
- There are bugs under my desk.
- The water in the hallway fountain is not cold enough.

Most of these are fair and appropriate questions. Some require more thought and planning than others do. With only the set of blueprints left by the architects and some rolls of trace, it took time to get back to the users with solutions to their problems.

It is obvious that many people do not like to wait. You cannot escape them; they find you in the elevators, hallways, and bathrooms. They even wait outside your office door to request their changes. There are two basic types of changes facility managers face every day:

1. Those that are necessary for valid business reasons. These are puzzles usually affecting adjacent groups. Having only some paper and a pencil meant it took time to explore ideas, review options, and implement decisions.

2. Those requested because employees did not want to sit where we put them, or they wanted to be on another floor closer to someone important. They usually prefaced this with "The chairman thinks it would be a good idea if our group moved." My answer was always "Is it OK if I discuss it with the chairman?" These questions would go away—but only after a struggle. While these were easier to answer, they always took longer to resolve and created the most stress.

In any line of business, when you cannot answer a question in a timely fashion, the person asking the question loses faith in your ability to perform. This was my biggest frustration and the beginning of my hope one day to be able to design a program that would enable facility managers to have information readily available and be able to answer questions in a timely manner.

Having said that, we did very well without the use of fax, mobile phone, email, text, instant message, Skype, etc. The reason was that we had no expectation that we would hear from the person for a while after their request. In today's world, people expect replies within minutes, and if we do not have a quick, accurate answer, they are upset.

Because I had the corporate experience, even though it was so long ago, it is now very easy to say that everyone planning to go into architecture, especially interior architecture, would benefit by spending a couple of years understanding how the corporate structure works. You learn how to deal with management on a daily basis and how to negotiate what the client looks for.

The main thing one learns working on the client side is that projects never end—they just transition to another phase. When the consultants are finished and go home, that is when the internal facilities group's work begins. There is "Life after Open House"—be prepared for it. Actually, starting new work is much more difficult than getting a building built in the first place.

Working for American Express was an unbelievable experience. In the last five years, it was fun traveling, mostly for two weeks at a time, to do projects in Mexico, England, France, and Italy, much to my wife's dismay, since she was left at home with two small kids.

Being a Strategic Thinker

I mentioned division's business plans in a prior section and the fact that most companies' business plans are really marketing plans addressing proposals for new products or services. Without knowing the corresponding staff increases or decreases associated with the business ideas, it is very difficult to anticipate or assist the groups from a real estate point of view. It's pretty clear that as a facility manager you have only two choices when it comes to helping the divisions project when an existing facility needs to be expanded or a new facility is needed:

1. Wait until the division yells, "Help, we need more space!"
2. Learn to help them get out in front of their need by working with them to anticipate their growth.

After the headquarters project was completed and I moved to a new position, my personal goal was to change the way the real estate department worked, from *always* being in a crisis mode to only *sometimes* being in a crisis mode.

In 1977, I was able to get my hands on an advance copy of the Card division's business plan and spent time analyzing how they wanted to grow the business. I knew how many departments there were in each facility, the number of staff in each department, their levels of work productivity, and the amount of space they occupied. I developed activity numbers for each department that related to departmental staffing and in short order created a matrix of the relationships between the number of units processed by a group to the number of people in that group and the amount of space they occupied.

That year, I was able to make recommendations as to when they should either expand existing facilities or build a new facility. It took an average of two to two and a half years to get a facility on line, so my information was very helpful. That led to my biggest achievement—being asked the following year to participate in each division's business planning meetings.

CHAPTER 17

Predictions for the Future
of the Profession

I think the future of an architectural practice will basically mirror what is happening in general business:

- Businesses will be more global.
- Larger firms will continue to get larger at the expense of the midsize firms.
- Clients will continue to reduce the number of vendors they work with and focus on those that act like strategic partners rather than just vendors.
- National contracts will be the norm, and single project contracts will be reduced.
- Architectural firms will need to be multidisciplined to be considered for corporate projects.
- Boutique firms will continue to be around for specialty projects.
- In ten years or so, most architectural firms may drop the word *architects* from their name.
- Related professionals—realtors, contractors, engineers, owner's reps, project managers—will continue to gobble up more of the nonliability services, leaving the liability services to architects, engineers, and contractors.
- Architectural services will be bid as commodities unless architects understand how to deliver value-based services.
- Nonarchitectural firms that have 3D modeling and design capabilities will be doing much of the initial project design work.
- Emailing will be significantly reduced, and other communication tools will be introduced that are more secure, can speed

up decision making, and are easier to archive and automatically erase. People may even go back to making telephone calls to improve communications.
- Open office design concepts will revert to more conventional offices to reduce noise levels, reduce sickness and absenteeism, increase ability to do private work, and increase privacy.
- Virtual reality presentations will become the norm.
- More staff will be working at home, at least part-time, reducing the need for leased space. Leased space will have more collaborative layouts and enclaves for private chats.
- Video conferencing, requiring sophisticated equipment, may become less popular, as meetings will be held in virtual offices on a laptop.
- Women in architecture will be more common, particularly in project management positions.
- Marketing will focus on ways to be better strategic partners.

Fortunately, I predict that the profession of architecture will still be around for many years. It may be somewhat changed, as indicated above, but it will still be an exciting, rewarding, and potentially lucrative career, whether you work for yourself or others.

I hope *Your Architecture Career* helps you to become more successful, whether you are just starting out, further along, or starting or even running your own firm. It is actually one of the most exciting times to be an architect. Technology may be changing the profession, but it is also opening up many possibilities for greater efficiencies as well as creative solutions for residential or commercial designs!

The way most of us meet today.

The way we will be meeting tomorrow. Will someone please turn off the lights—the meeting is over!

List of Terms

accrual method: The accrual method of accounting records income when earned or billed and records expenses when incurred.

addendum: A supplement to documents, issued prior to taking receipt of bids, for the purpose of clarifying, correcting, or otherwise changing bid documents previously issued.

additional services: Services provided in addition to those specifically designated as basic services in an agreement between the owner and CM. Also known as Supplemental Services.

agenda: Usually prepared prior to a meeting listing points to be discussed; sometimes refers to the list of topics itself.

agreement: A document setting forth the relationships and obligations between two parties, such as the CM and owner or contractor and owner. It may incorporate other documents by reference.

AIA: The American Institute of Architects is a professional organization for licensed architects in the United States.

amenities: Amenities are the enhancements that buildings offer tenants. These may include a security desk, health club, garage, fitness center, conference center, cafeteria, children's playroom, common lounge, etc.

American Express: The American Express Company, also known as Amex, is an American multinational financial services company.

app: Software designed to run on smartphones and other mobile devices.

apparent low bidder: The bidder who has submitted the lowest bid for a division of work described in bid documents, a proposal form, or a proposed contract.

approval: As in client giving their written approval of a task, concept, or phase of the work

approved bidders list: List of contractors who have been prequalified for the purpose of submitting responsible, competitive bids.

approved changes: Changes in the contract documents that have been subjected to an agreed-upon change approval process and have been approved by the party empowered to approve such changes.

architect: A tradesman who designs and produces plans for buildings, often overseeing the building process. An architect is someone who plans, designs, and reviews the construction of buildings.

as-built drawings: Architectural drawings (plans) that show the completed work, as actually installed. Also known as Record Drawings.

ASID: The American Society of Interior Designers (ASID) is the largest professional organization for interior designers. Of the Society's 20,000 practicing interior designers, 6,500 practice primarily in the commercial field, and 4,000 practice primarily as residential designers. The remaining 9,500 work in both commercial and residential design.

awarded project: When a client selects a firm to assist them on an architectural assignment, the architectural firm calls the "win" an awarded project.

bid: Response by a vendor to perform a specified body of work as described in a proposal or RFP.

bid documents: The documents issued to the contractor(s) by the owner, which describe the proposed work and contract terms. Bid documents typically include drawings, specifications, contract forms, general and supplementary conditions, proposal or bid forms, and other information.

bidding: The process of getting prices from consultants, contractors, and/ or subcontractors, usually based on an RFP or set of completed documents referred to as construction documents, including plans, material lists, details, and specifications.

billing: A sum of monthly invoices consultants send to clients listing all project costs based on a time basis, lump sum basis, or percentage of construction costs. Invoices also include a list of all reimbursable expenses. The sum of all consultants' monthly invoices is the monthly billing for a firm.

blocking: A graphical representation of departments and functions planned for a floor.

Blueprint for Savings: A product, designed by CPG Architects, to assist building owners in efficiently attracting prospective tenants to their building.

blueprints: Architectural plans for a building or construction project, which are likely to include floor plans, footing and foundation plans, elevations, plot plans, and various schedules or details.

BOMA: The Building Owners and Managers Association (BOMA) is a professional organization for commercial real estate professionals based in the United States and Canada. Membership includes building owners, managers, developers, architects, leasing professionals, corporate facility managers, asset managers, and the providers of products and services needed to operate commercial properties.

branding (personal): Personal branding is the practice of people marketing themselves and their careers as brands. It is the ongoing process of establishing a prescribed image or impression in the minds of others about an individual, group, or organization. Personal branding often involves the application of one's name to various products.

budget: The dollar amount allocated by the owner for a project or program.

building department: A department within a city, township, or county government with qualified staff to make professional judgments about whether a building meets building code requirements.

building permit: Written authorization from the city, county, or other governing regulatory body, usually called the building department, giving permission to construct or renovate a building. A building permit is specific to the building project described in the application.

CAD: Computer Aided Drafting (CAD) is the use of computer systems to aid in the creation, modification, analysis, or optimization of drawings for building projects. CAD software is used to increase the productivity of the designer and improve communications of professionals who share documents. CAD output is often in the form of electronic files for file or print.

CAP X: Capital Expenditures (CAP X) is the preparation and summary of capital projects planned for the next calendar year. Architects, engineers, and contractors in conjunction with corporate real estate and facilities managers prepare CAP X budgets.

capital improvement: Capital improvement is an item that adds value to a property, adapts the property to new uses, or prolongs the life of property. Capital improvement projects are typically depreciated, while maintenance projects are typically expensed.

career path: The path one takes in his or her career, often assisted by career counselors or guidance counselors.

cash flow: Operating cash flows are those related to a company's operations, that is, its day-to-day business.

cash method: The cash method of accounting records revenue when cash is received, and expenses when they are paid.

Certificate of Occupancy (C of O): The Certificate of Occupancy is a certificate issued by a local governmental entity responsible for the use of land and buildings in the community where the property is located. The C of O states that the structures on the property or any improvements made to these structures comply with the codes, ordinances, and regulations of that governmental entity and that they may be occupied.

change order: Written agreement or directive between contracted parties that represents an addition, deletion, or revision to the original contract. A change order identifies a change in price and time and describes the nature (scope) of the work involved.

changed conditions: Conditions or circumstances, physical or otherwise, that alter the conditions or circumstances on which the original contract documents were based.

checklist: A checklist is a type of informational job aid, a "to-do" list, reminding a user not to forget important tasks. A checklist helps to ensure consistency and completeness in carrying out a task.

churn: As used in this book, churn is the process of redoing previously prepared (and often approved by the client) work.

closeout: The process, after the client has moved into a building, of describing all the operational elements in the building to property management. Closeout items may include systems such as mechanical, electrical, plumbing, fire protection, emergency power, security, audiovisual, lighting, etc. It is the last phase in a construction project and includes copies of all as-built construction documents, product warranties, and guarantees.

CM fee: A form of contractual payment for services, where the CM, construction manager, is paid a fee for services performed.

code: As in building code, listing all the requirements of construction. Codes are based on building size, type of construction, use, and occupancy and often vary according to jurisdiction.

commissioning: Start-up, calibration, and certification of a facility. See Closeout.

CONNSTEP: CONNSTEP is a business consulting firm, helping manufacturers and other businesses with strategic leadership and operational methodologies that make the company more competitive in today's challenging economic climate. CONNSTEP consultants provide business and technical solutions that help others to grow strategically, improve profitability, and create sustainable competitive advantages in the marketplace.

construction budget: The sum of all costs of anticipated items of work. The total construction budget often includes a design contingency, contractor's fee, general conditions, and insurance.

construction contract documents: Agreed-to documents that provide the basis for a contract entered into between parties. They typically include the bid documents updated to reflect the agreement between the owner and the contractor(s).

construction documents (CDs): A set of plans, specifications, material descriptions, and details prepared for a contractor to construct a building.

construction loan: A loan provided by a lending institution specifically to construct or renovate a building.

construction management: A professional management practice consisting of an array of services applied to construction projects and programs through the planning, design, construction, and postconstruction phases for the purpose of achieving project objectives including the management of quality, cost, time, and scope.

construction manager (CM): A professional construction manager (CM) acts as an extension of staff to the owner and manages the entire project. A CM assists with preplanning, design, construction, engineering, and management expertise that can assure the best possible project outcome no matter what type of project delivery method used. A CM is not a general contractor. The term construction manager is often used interchangeably with project manager.

construction observation: The process whereby architects, engineers, and other professionals observe the work of the contractors to make sure they are performing the construction according to the construction plans and specifications.

construction schedule: A graphic, tabular, or narrative representation or depiction of the time of construction of the project, showing activities and duration of activities in sequential order.

contingency: A contingency is an amount included in a construction budget to cover any unforeseen conditions.

contract: An agreement between two or more people that creates a legal obligation to do or not do a particular thing.

contractor: The organization or individual who undertakes responsibility for the performance of the work, in accordance with plans, specifications, and contract documents, providing and controlling the labor, material, and equipment to accomplish the work.

Co-Opetition: The title of a book by Adam M. Brandenburger and Barry J. Nalebuff describing the way firms sometimes compete with one another on a project and at other times are complementary with one another.

cover letter: As used in this book, a letter introducing a person with their professional qualifications to a prospective employer.

CPG Architects: CPG Architects is an architectural firm, founded in 1980 by Gary Unger, headquartered in Stamford, CT. (Originally called The Corporate Planning Group, the name was changed to CPG Architects a few years later.)

CPM: The Critical Path Method (CPM) is a scheduling technique used to plan and control a project. CPM combines all relevant information into a single visual representation defining the sequence and duration of operations, and depicting the interrelationship of the work elements required to complete the project.

CRS: Caudill Rowlett Scott Architects (CRS) was founded in Houston and currently, after a number of mergers and acquisitions, is part of HOK Architects (formerly Hellmuth Obata + Kassabaum).

culture: Corporate culture refers to the beliefs and behaviors that determine how a company's employees and management interact and handle outside business transactions. Often, corporate culture is implied, not expressly defined, and develops organically over time from the cumulative traits of the people the company hires.

database: Information captured in spreadsheets or software applications that can be integrated to produce reports, charts, and graphs.

design development: The phase of architects' work where design details are being worked out, materials selected, and furniture selected for review by client.

designer: The individual or organization that performs the design and prepares plans and specifications for the work to be performed. The designer can be an architect, an engineer, or an organization that combines professional services.

disruptor: For the purpose of this book, a disruptor is a person or firm who welcomes the challenge of introducing new ideas and services that can positively affect the profession in terms of profitability, image, and growth.

drafting: A term used to describe the manual method of drawing, prior to CAD. Often called mechanical drawing. The architect worked with either a T-square or parallel bar to prepare drawings.

efficiency: When referenced from a space point of view, it is the ratio of usable space to total rented space. The difference, presented in terms of percentage, is the efficiency of the space. When referenced from an operations point of view, it is the measurement of the time spent on an issue compared to the time allocated.

elevation: A drawing or photo of the side of a building.

entrepreneur: A person who organizes and operates a business or businesses, taking on greater than normal financial risks in order to do so.

envisioning: The name of the first phase of an architectural project where the client is asked general questions about the company's goals and objectives in terms of culture, workflow, staffing, growth, equipment needs, and facility objectives of light, color, and workplace standards.

estimated cost to complete: The current estimate of the remaining costs to be incurred on a project.

estimated final cost: The anticipated cost of a project or project element when it is complete. The sum of all project costs such as construction, fees for consultants, furniture, IT, AV, security, branding elements, and relocation costs.

ethics: Moral principles that govern a person's behavior. Each firm sets standards for employee behavior.

façade: Normally the primary elevation and front of a building.

facility management: Facility management is a profession that encompasses multiple disciplines to ensure functionality of the built environment by integrating people, place, process, and technology. Facility Management is also a class of software used by facilities managers to manage and report on space, people, furniture, and equipment.

fast track: The process of dividing the design of a project into phases in such a manner as to permit construction to start before the entire design phase is complete. The overlapping of the construction phase with the design phases.

field order: An order issued at the site by the owner or CM to clarify and/or require the contractor(s) to perform work not included in the contract documents. A field order normally represents a minor change not involving a change in contract price or time and may or may not be the basis of a change order.

final design: The stage of the design process when drawings and specifications are completed for construction bid purposes. It is preceded by the preliminary design stage, and followed by the procurement phase. The designation used by designers for the last part of the design process prior to procurement.

floor plan: The basic layout of a building, an interior expansion, renovation, or addition, including placement of walls, windows, and doors as well as dimensions.

general conditions: A section of general clauses in the contract specifications that establish how the project is to be administered. Included are obligations such as providing temporary work, insurance, field offices, etc.

gross lease: A gross lease is a lease in which the lessor pays all costs of operating and maintaining the property, including the property taxes.

guaranteed maximum price: A contractual form of agreement wherein a maximum price for the work is established based on an agreed-upon scope.

handoff: A handoff occurs when responsibility for a phase passes from one person to another or from one firm to another.

HVAC: HVAC is an acronym that stands for heating, ventilation, and air conditioning.

IFMA: The International Facility Management Association (IFMA) is the world's largest and most recognized international association for facility management professionals.

innovator: An innovator is a person who introduces new methods, ideas, or products.

interior designer: An interior designer is someone who plans, researches, coordinates, and manages interior design projects. Interior design is a multifaceted profession that includes conceptual development, space planning, site inspections, programming, and research, communicating with the stakeholders of a project, construction management, and execution of the design. Interior design is the process of shaping the experience of interior space, through the manipulation of spatial volume as well as surface treatment, for the betterment of human functionality.

internship: An internship is job training for white-collar and professional careers.

intrapreneur: Those who take hands-on responsibility for creating innovation of any kind within a business, as opposed to the entrepreneur, who often starts businesses.

job search: As used in this book, the process of looking for a part-time or full-time position in an architectural or interior design firm.

license: In the case of architecture, each state requires candidates to "appren-tice" for a specific period of time before they can take the licensing exam. Upon passing the exam, the candidate becomes registered by the state to sign and seal drawings for construction.

"life after open house": An expression coined by Gary Unger in 1982 stating that "life goes on after an architectural project is completed." Architects should understand there is an opportunity to continue to work with that client offering follow-up services.

life cycle: As used in this book, services designed to assist the client during their entire occupation of a facility. These services include not just the initial architectural services of planning and design, but also after move-in services to include lease administration, facility anagement, maintenance and WorkOrder, and finally circling back to services for new planning and design opportunities.

life cycle cost: Life cycle costs include all costs incident to the planning, design, construction, operation, maintenance, and demolition of a facility, or system, for a given life expectancy, all in terms of present value.

LINK5: A software program written by CPG Architects to manage and track internal contacts, potential projects, awarded projects, timesheets, and billing and reporting.

long lead items: Items that may have an extended delivery time and that may be considered for early procurement and purchase. Items that may be delivered too late for timely installation if their procurement or purchase were included as part of the procurement for the entire contract or project.

long-range planning: An architectural service for clients to assist in the analysis and projection of business, people, and space needs for the purpose of determining requirements for new facilities.

low bidder: The bidder who has submitted the lowest approved bid, which is determined to be responsive and responsible for a division of work described in a bid document, proposal form, or contract.

marketing (firm): Firm marketing, sometimes called firm branding, includes things the firm and employees can do to drive new business and enhance the reputation of the firm.

marketing (personal): Personal marketing, sometimes called personal branding, includes things individuals can do to enhance their personal brand and make themselves more valuable to the firm.

master schedule: An executive-level summary identifying the major components of a project, their sequence, and durations. The schedule can be in the form of a Network diagram, Milestone Schedule, or Bar Chart. Software programs like SmartSheet and Microsoft Project are examples of applications used by professionals.

mentoring: A professional relationship in which a person assists another in developing specific skills and knowledge that will enhance the other person's professional and personal growth.

MEP: Mechanical, Electrical, and Plumbing Engineers. In addition to the architect, these engineers are prime consultants on most projects.

metrics: Standards of measurement by which efficiency, performance, progress, or quality of a plan, process, or product can be assessed.

milestone schedule: A schedule representing important events along the path to project completion. Not all milestones may be equally significant. The most significant are termed "major milestones" and usually represent the completion of a group of activities.

move-in: The phase after a tenant takes possession of a property. Move-in can happen simultaneously with receiving the Certificate of Occupancy (C of O).

notice of award: A formal document informing an individual or organization of successfully securing a contract.

open-plan office: A floor plan design where most of the occupants work "in the open" rather in semiprivate or private offices. Occupants may work in cubicles, workstations, or benching tables.

owner's rep: An owner's representative is typically a third party (individual or company) that is hired by the owner or tenant to represent them during site selection, design, and construction phases as well as relocation.

plot plan: A bird's-eye view showing how a building sits on the building lot, typically showing setbacks (how far the building must sit from the road), easements, rights of way, and drainage.

pre-lease: The first phase of an architect's work in an interior design project that includes site selection, programming, lease and building analysis, test fits, and preparation of preliminary budgets and schedules.

preliminary design: Also known as design development. The transition from the schematic phase to the completion of the design development. During this phase, ancillary space is developed and dimensions are finalized. Outline specifications are developed into technical specifications, sections are delineated, and elevations are defined.

prequalification: A prequalification is a process in which a loan officer calculates the housing-to-income ratio and the total debt-to-income ratio to determine an approximate maximum mortgage loan amount.

principal: A person with responsibility to commit a firm financially and contractually. Similar title to partner, owner, founder, etc.

programming: The phase of an architectural or interior design project where the architect meets with the client to determine their project goals and objectives, and business, staff, and space requirements.

project budget: The sum or target figure established to cover all the owner's costs of the project. It includes the cost of construction and all other costs such as land, legal and professional fees, interest, and other project-related costs.

project manager: The person in overall charge of the planning and execution of a particular project.

ProLease: Lease administration software, FASB compliant, used by over 800 large corporations to manage their leased and owned properties.

punch list: A list made near the completion of the construction work indicating items of work that remain unfinished, do not meet quality or quantity requirements as specified, or are yet to be performed by the contractor prior to completing the terms of the contract.

REBNY: The Real Estate Board of New York (REBNY) is a trade association for the real estate industry. The board works to promote industry-backed policies.

repeat business: When a customer returns to purchase goods or services from a business.

résumé: A résumé is a document used by a person to present their backgrounds and skills for a potential job.

RFI: A request for information (RFI) is a standard business process whose purpose is to collect written information about the capabilities of various suppliers.

RFP: A request for proposal (RFP) is a document that solicits proposal, often made through a bidding process, by an agency or company interested in procurement of a commodity, service, or valuable asset, to potential suppliers to submit business proposals.

schematic design: The first stage of the designer's basic services. In the schematic stage, the designer ascertains the requirements of the project and prepares schematic design studies consisting of drawings and other documents illustrating the scale and relationships of the project.

scope changes: Changes that expand or reduce the requirements of the project during design or construction.

shop drawings: Drawings typically prepared by the contractor, based upon the contract documents and provided in sufficient detail, that indicate to the designer that the contractor intends to construct the referenced work in a manner that is consistent with the design intent and the contract documents.

SketchUp: SketchUp is 3-D modeling software that is easy to download.

snow cards: The snow card technique is a brainstorming tool that allows groups to share individual ideas about a project. The cards are often pinned to a wall in categories or themes.

specifications: The detailed written descriptions of materials, equipment, systems, and required workmanship and other qualitative information pertaining to the work.

spreadsheet: An electronic document in which data are arranged in the rows and columns of a grid and can be manipulated and used in calculations. Microsoft Excel is one example of a spreadsheet program.

square footage: The area measured in square feet of a certain property. Square footage can be measured in different ways and is usually considered approximate. "Usable Square Feet" (USF) describes the actual area occupied from wall to wall; USF does not include common areas of a building such as lobbies, restrooms, stairwells, storage rooms (unless used by only one tenant), building mechanical spaces, and shared hallways. "Rentable square feet" (RSF) includes the usable area, plus the tenants' proportional share of the common areas.

squatters: Squatters is an expression coined by CRS Architects referencing an architectural team that occupies a room in a client's facility for a short time while working with a client to plan conceptual design for a project.

stacking: A stacking plan refers to the vertical distribution and relationships of departments in a company, throughout the floors of a building. Also see Blocking.

storyboard: A storyboard is a graphic representation of how your ideas of an architectural project will unfold, drawing by drawing. It is made up of a number of squares with illustrations or pictures representing each plan or detail required for that plan. It may contain notes about important facts to remember.

strategic partner: A strategic partner is an individual or a firm that provides exceptional service to a corporation and may be awarded projects without competitive bidding.

strategic thinker: Strategic thinking goes beyond looking at what is—it involves imagining what could be. It is a person with a fresh point of view on a market, a unique take on the future, or a capacity to imagine new answers to old problems. It is a person who is most interested in "what comes *after* what comes next."

subcontractor: A contractor who has a contract with a prime contractor to perform work.

supplementary general conditions: Additions and/or modifications to the general conditions, which are part of the bid documents and/or contract documents.

test fits: Developers, brokers, and potential tenants of interior spaces can use test fits in order to test the feasibility of a potential space before committing to it. Architects or interior designers usually prepare test fits.

Think 360: Thinking about the life cycle services an architect can provide for the life of a project. Think 360 is a holistic thought process, wherein one observes patterns from the past to gain a better understanding about the present. All of this serves to produce better decisions in the future.

value engineering: The process of either selecting a different material or product or identifying a better way to do something in order to reduce the cost.

vendor: Anyone who provides goods or services to a company or individuals.

virtual reality: A person using virtual reality equipment is able to "look around" the artificial world, and with high quality VR move about in it, and interact with features or items depicted in the headset. Virtual reality is displayed with a virtual reality headset. VR headsets are head-mounted goggles with a screen in front of the eyes. Programs may include audio through speakers or headphones.

workplace: The workplace is the physical location where someone works for his or her living. Such a place can range from a home office to a large office building or factory.

workplace solution: Workplace solutions experts help you achieve productivity improvement targets.

workplace strategy: Workplace strategy is the study of organizations' work patterns for the purpose of reducing or reallocating costs to be able to manage more efficiently. A common goal is to increase employee productivity and reduce real estate costs.

workstation: An area where work of a particular nature is carried out, such as a specific location in an office or at home.

Bibliography

Allen, David. *Getting Things Done.* Revised edition. New York: Penguin Books, 2015.

Brandenburger, Adam M. and Barry J. Nalebuff. *Co-Opetition.* New York: Doubleday, 1997.

Christian, Brian and Tom Griffiths. *Algorithms to Live By: The Computer Science of Human Decisions.* New York: Holt, 2016.

Ferriss, Timothy. *The 4-Hour Workweek.* New York: Harmony, 2009.

Fried, Jason and David Heinemeier Hansson. *Remote.* New York: Crown, 2013.

Froggatt, Cynthia C. *Work Naked.* San Francisco: Jossey-Bass, 2001.

Gallo, Carmine. *The Storyteller's Secret: From TED Speakers to Business Legends, Why Some Ideas Catch On and Others Don't.* New York: St. Martin's Press, 2016.

Gladwell, Malcolm. *Blink.* New York: Back Bay Books/Little Brown, 2007.

Grant, Adam. *Originals: How Non-Conformists Move the World.* New York: Viking Press, 2016.

Heath, Chip and Dan Heath. *Made to Stick.* New York: Random House, 2007.

Meyer, Danny. *Setting the Table.* New York: Harper, 2008.

Peña, William M., FAIA, and Steven A. Parshall, FAIA. *Problem Seeking: An Architectural Programming Primer (5th edition)* Hoboken, NJ: Wiley, 2012.

Pollak, Lindsey. *Becoming the Boss: New Rules for the Next Generation of Leaders.* New York: HarperBusiness, 2014.

Ramo, Joshua Copper. *The Seventh Sense.* New York: Little Brown, 2016.

Rockefeller, J. D. *The Life and Style of Sir Richard Branson.* Createspace, 2016.

Sinek, Simon. *Leaders Eat Last.* New York: Portfolio, 2014.

Wang, R "Ray." *Disrupting Digital Business.* Cambridge, MA: Harvard Business Review Press, 2015.

White, Shira P. and G. Patton Wright. *New Ideas about New Ideas.* New York: Basic Books, 2002.

Suggested Readings

Here are a few of my favorite reads:

The 4-Hour Workweek: Escape 9–5, Live Anywhere, and Join the New Rich by Timothy Ferriss (Harmony, 2009)

Algorithms to Live By: The Computer Science of Human Decisions by Brian Christian and Tom Griffiths (Henry Holt and Co., 2016)

Art's Principles: 50 Years of Hard-Learned Lessons in Builing a World-Class Professional Services Firm by Arthur Gensler with Michael Lindenmayer (Wilson Lafferty, 2015)

Badass Your Brand: The Impatient Entrepreneur's Guide to Turning Expertise into Profit by Pia Silva (Worstofall Design, 2017)

Becoming the Boss: New Rules for the Next Generation of Leaders by Lindsey Pollak (HarperBusiness, 2014)

Blink: The Power of Thinking without Thinking by Malcolm Gladwell (Little, Brown and Company, 2005)

Co-Opetition by Adam M. Brandenburger and Barry J. Nalebuff (Doubleday Business, 1996)

Disrupting Digital Business: Create an Authentic Experience in the Peer-to-Peer Economy by R. "Ray" Wang (Harvard Business Review Press, 2015)

Getting Things Done: The Art of Stress-Free Productivity by David Allen (Penguin Books, 2015)

Leaders Eat Last: Why Some Teams Pull Together and Others Don't by Simon Sinek (Portfolio, 2017)

The Life and Style of Sir Richard Branson by J.D. Rockefeller (CreateSpace Independent Publishing, 2016)

Made to Stick: Why Some Ideas Survive and Others Die by Chip Heath and Dan Heath (Random House, 2007)

New Ideas about New Ideas by Shira P. White and G. Patton Wright (Basic Books, 2002)

Originals: How Non-Conformists Move the World by Adam Grant (Viking, 2016)

Problem Seeking: An Architectural Programming Primer (5th Edition) by William M. Peña and Steven A. Parshall (Wiley, 2012)

Remote: Office Not Required by Jason Fried and David Heinemeier Hansson (Crown Business, 2013)

Setting the Table: The Transforming Power of Hospitality in Business by Danny Meyer (Harper, 2006)

The Seventh Sense: Power, Fortune, and Survival in the Age of Networks by Joshua Cooper Ramo (Little, Brown and Company, 2016)

The Storyteller's Secret: From TED Speakers to Business Legends, Why Some Ideas Catch On and Others Don't by Carmine Gallo (St. Martin's Press, 2016)

Work Naked: Eight Essential Principles for Peak Performance in the Virtual Workplace by Cynthia C. Froggatt (Jossey-Bass, 2001)

Resources

ACSA—Association Collegiate Schools of Architecture
AECB—Association for Environmentally Conscious Buildings
AIA—American Institute of Architects (There are 260 AIA chapters around the
    world.)
AIA Continuing Education Program
AIAS—American Institute of Architecture Students
American Architectural Foundation
American Society of Landscape Architects
ASID—American Association of Interior Designers
Canadian Architecture
CMAA—Construction Management Association of America
FMC—Facility Management Student Chapter
IFMA—International Facilities Manager Association
IIDA—International Interior Design Association
National Council of Architectural Registration Boards
Royal Institute of Architects

About the Author

Gary Unger started his architectural studies at Washington University in St. Louis but finished up at the University of Texas at Austin. After graduation, he headed east to New York City. After working for CRS Architects and American Express, Gary started his own architectural firm in 1980, CPG Architects. In 1990, he started a real estate software business, Link Systems. The company's first software product was Facility Management—providing services to clients after the architectural project was completed. CPG Architects and Link Systems are based in Stamford, Connecticut. CPG has done thousands of projects for clients including General Electric, Snapple, Nestlé, Newman's Own, Dannon Yogurt, and Bridgewater. Twenty-six years later, Link Systems has 5 major enterprise applications for corporations including: Lease Management, Equipment Management, Facility Management, Maintenance/WorkOrder, and Portfolio Management, servicing almost 1,000 clients. Recently, Gary was named Real Estate Person of the Year by the March of Dimes. For more on Gary's companies, please go to: http://www.cpgarch.com and http://www.linksystems.com or to his personal website at http://www.GaryUnger42.com.

Gary is one of the very lucky ones who made it in a profession described by many as being "a tough place to make a buck." His career has been exciting and extremely rewarding. It would be hard for anyone to "plan for" the types of experiences he has had. His career included four distinct buckets of experience—where each experience built on the prior one:

1. First, having phenomenal summer jobs, and not realizing their importance until later.
2. Second, working at CRS Architects and American Express—two very different companies.
3. Third, the experience of starting an architectural business "from scratch"—CPG Architects, 1980.
4. Fourth, the experience of starting a real estate software business "from scratch"—Link Systems, 1990.

His wife says his fifth bucket can be whatever he wants, as long as it does not include lunch at home.

Index

Books from Allworth Press

Brand Thinking and Other Noble Pursuits
by Debbie Millman with Rob Walker (6 × 9, 336 pages, paperback, $19.95)

Business and Legal Forms for Interior Designers
by Tad Crawford and Eva Doman Bruck (8½ × 11, 288 pages, paperback, $29.95)

Corporate Creativity
by Thomas Lockwood and Thomas Walton (6 × 9, 256 pages, paperback, $24.95)

Emotional Branding
by Marc Gobe (6 × 9, 352 pages, paperback, $19.95)

From Idea to Exit
by Jeffrey Weber (6 × 9, 272 pages, paperback, $19.95)

Green Interior Design
by Lori Dennis (8½ × 10, 160 pages, paperback, $24.95)

Infectious
by Achim Nowak (5½ × 8¼, 224 pages, paperback, $19.95)

Intentional Leadership
by Jane A. G. Kise (7 × 10, 224 pages, paperback, $19.95)

Legal Forms for Everyone (Sixth Edition)
by Carl W. Battle (8½ × 11, 280 pages, paperback, $24.99)

Legal Guide to Social Media
by Kimberly A. Houser (6 × 9, 208 pages, paperback, $19.95)

Millennial Rules
by T. Scott Gross (6 × 9, 176 pages, paperback, $16.95)

Peak Business Performance Under Pressure
by Bill Driscoll and Peter Joffre Nye with John McCain (6 × 9, 224 pages, paperback, $19.95)

The Pocket Small Business Owner's Guide to Business Plans
by Brian Hill and Dee Power (5¼ × 8¼, 224 pages, paperback, $14.95)

Positively Outrageous Service
by T. Scott Gross (6 × 9, 224 pages, paperback, $19.99)

Star Brands
by Carolina Rogoll with Debbie Millman (6 × 9, 256 pages, paperback, $24.99)

The Ultimate Guide to Internships
by Eric Woodard (6 × 9, 280 pages, paperback, $14.99)

Website Branding for Small Businesses
by Nathalie Nahai (6 × 9, 288 pages, paperback, $19.95)

To see our complete catalog or to order online, please visit www.allworth.com.

Notes

Notes

Notes

Notes

Notes

Notes

Notes

Notes

Notes

Notes

Notes

Notes

Notes

Notes